Up McHenry Creek Without a Paddle

The Bodacious Fishing Adventures of a Simple Man from Rural Arkansas

Terry Bryant

Copyright © 2017 Terry Bryant
All rights reserved
First Edition
PAGE PUBLISHING, INC.
New York, NY
First originally published by Page Publishing, Inc. 2017
ISBN 978-1-64082-200-9 (Paperback)
ISBN 978-1-64082-201-6 (Digital)
Printed in the United States of America

Copyright © 2018 Terry Bryant

All right reserved

2nd Edition

If you enjoy this book:

Please consider checking out my latest title!

Traveling for Terry Bryant is an unpredictable adventure...or misadventure rather.

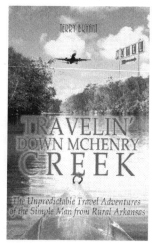

The business of training people on how to be safe in their work environment has taken him near and far. He has run the gamut in his attitude from being angry about the randomness of traveling to savoring the variety.

At some point, among the urine-soaked mattresses, two to be exact, and unexpected naked ladies in his room, Terry found a way to experience joy in the unpredictable nature of air travel and budget motels.

In addition, Terry has survived a knife fight, been detained at a military base, and managed to navigate an uncomfortable confrontation with a couple of booze-soaked honeymooners.

Terry's stories both delight and empower. From the first chapter, you will gain a new, positive perspective from a man who turns the strife of life into a wild and exciting adventure.

Do not miss these, and many more fun and hilarious stories courtesy of the simple man from rural Arkansas.

Grab it on your favorite reading platform by clicking this link - http://mchenrycreekfishers.com/travelingmchenrycreek

Table of Contents

Preface

Every outdoorsman has had one or two misadventures—I've made a living!

I have:

Fallen out of a boat eleven times. (Some caused visits to the ER.)

Broken an arm falling into my boat. (January 2016)

Broken an arm falling out of boat. (Young and stupid.)

Broken ribs attempting to get to boat. (No comment.)

Lost motor off the boat four times. (Uh, well, uh, you know.)

Lost boat trailer from the truck multiple times. (In four different decades.)

Had my head stuck in the mud at the bottom of a lake. (Don't try it alone.)

Fished all day with a lure stuck in my head. (You get used to it.)

Bitten by a cottonmouth moccasin on one trip. (Yeah, that's exciting.)

Once paddled my boat with a hubcap. (Well, who hasn't.)

My first aid kit consists of duct tape! (Don't leave home without it.)

My bio reads as follows:

Rushed to emergency room twenty times. (Zero car wrecks.)

More than twenty broken bones. (All from fishing, hunting, and ball playing.)

Over one hundred stitches. (Never been in a knife fight.)

Multiple concussions. (Obviously.)

One snake bite. (The devil was trying to kill me.)

One wife. (And she's getting tired of it.)

Everything in the following account is true. In order for this adventure to continue, you need to start reading, and I'll keep fishing. Or you can go on a trip with me. Bring a camera!

(Pssst, the password is 911!)

* * * * *

I've been a fisherman all my life. You know my type. Our favorite bumper sticker is "Eat, Sleep, Go Fishin'." Our favorite button says, "Bad day fishing is better than a good day at work." And then there is this ad, "Wanted: New Wife with Boat and Motor. Please send picture of boat and motor." I've got it so bad that some Saturdays, I hook up to my boat knowing I'm not going fishing! I pull it to my office where I might just be catching up on a few things or working on this book or running a few errands. It just makes me feel good to be hooked up.

Mid-February 2016

My eighty-two-year-old dad: Did you catch any?

Me: Haven't been fishing.

Dad: I saw you pulling your boat the other day.

Me: I was catching up on some work at my office.

Dad: Why would you hook up to your boat just to tow it around?

Me: Makes me feel good.

Dad: Are you stupid?

Me: I don't understand the question.

Fishing is a disease that has afflicted my family for five generations now. My mom used fishhooks for diaper pins. Our dad whipped us with an old broken fishing rod. (They were always handy.) Most kids wanted toys for Christmas. My brothers and I were hoping for a small-lipped minnow lure, spinner bait, plastic worms, or some other fishing tackle to go after the many fish in McHenry Creek that were no match for us. I remember watching the Saturday Major League game of the week on TV with my grandfather. I would watch the baseball game, and he would doze on the couch. As he snored away, every once in a while, you could hear him talking in his sleep. Just broken sentences about "bass" or

"Shannon spinner" or "lunkers."

I can still see my nephew at seven or eight years old, walking McHenry Creek next to my parents' house the minute after he and his dad had returned from fishing all day at Maumelle or Harris Brake or some other lake where they had caught fish all day. He was possessed to catch a few more before it got too dark. The only e-mail address he has ever had is onemorecast@——. Twenty-five years later, his five-year-old son is showing signs of the illness already. (Hey, even our dog once caught a fish! See chapter 8.)

I remember my first Zebco 33. Man, what a reel. A friend I fished with named mine "ole grinder." Something to do with the sound it made during use. (Of course, it sounded like that. It was worn out from catching so many fish.) He and I spent most every Saturday fishing McHenry or a few ponds in the area. I can still vividly remember grabbing our poles, jumping on our bikes, and pedaling as fast as we could to Mr. Young's gate where we would throw down our bikes and run to the creek trying to catch the first one of the day. Fishing is a passion, and we had it bad. Little did I know that something so simple and harmless could end up in adventurous disasters.

I have lived on McHenry Creek my entire life. In elementary school in the early sixties, my friends and brothers and I would ride bikes down the road from our house about a mile and walk the bank of McHenry for hours fishing. It was considered "day care" before we ever heard of the phrase.

During my teen years, my folks built a house on the back of my great-grandparents' old homeplace. At the very back of our three acres, McHenry Creek literally sprang up out of the ground. We could find old pieces of wooden barrel and piping where my great-granddad and his son, Uncle Heavy, would make moonshine beside the bubbling spring. One of our uncles had a bulldozer, and he and my dad dug out a small pond that we swam in and stocked with fish. It stayed clear due to the fact that McHenry began at the upper end of it and flowed through it.

My parents bought a ten-acre plot and built a house on the bank of McHenry in the late seventies. It is a few miles downstream from our previous home. They still live there. Our grandparents even built a house across the road from McHenry Creek in the early sixties. When my wife and I got married, we rented a small trailer on the bank of McHenry. After a few years, we built a house on a hill and moved in, in 1986. In the winter, I can look out the kitchen window, down the hill, and see the bridge crossing McHenry that we travel every day. She even agreed that we "might" name our first son McHenry. We have two daughters, so I never found out if she was serious. I even painted the words McHenry Creek on the side of my boat—by hand, of course. McHenry Creek is the main constant in my family's existence.

This obsession with fishing has led to numerous experiences. Many of these experiences have turned into adventures. Many of these adventures have turned into disasters and disasters into catastrophes and, well, you get the idea. As an example, I have experienced two experience-adventure-disaster-catastrophes   recently. On July 31, 2015, one of my brothers and I were wade-fishing a creek in north Arkansas catching smallmouth. I slipped on a slick rock and fell backward onto the edge of the bank. I threw my arms back to catch myself and landed on a cottonmouth moccasin. He bit me on the right arm just below the elbow. I was released from the hospital three days later (chapter 10). And I fell and broke my right arm on a fishing trip on January 2, 2016. (If anything, else happens before the book is finished, I will add it here.) Well, it happened again! (Broken bone on back of left hand, early June 2016.)

When I was about twelve, I saved a few dollars and gave it to my mom, so she could order me a subscription for a hunting and fishing magazine. They had a section every month titled, "This Happened to Me." It was the first section I turned to as soon as the magazine would arrive in the mail. It was someone's firsthand account of a calamity that had happened to them while on some outdoor adventure. As I became an adult, I realized I was living these adventures regularly.

Most children were told by their mother, "You're an accident waiting to happen." Everyone's heard that. My mom expressed it a little differently, "You're an accident looking for a place to happen." It fits. You read my bio in the description. All these came from ball playing, hunting, and fishing—and I don't drink!

I have been battling serious osteoarthritis in both knees

and ankles for many years now, probably due to my chosen lifestyle of playing hard. My doctor calls it the "rode hard and put up wet" kind of arthritis. That fits. In 2014 when one of my friends saw me on crutches for the first time, he reminded me that "when you live your life in a four-wheel drive, this is how you end up." People ask me, now that I know the results of living life with reckless abandon would end up with my being crippled, would I have changed anything? Yes. If this is as bad as it gets, I would have played harder!

I have decided that I better start recording these things that happened over my sixty-two years of existence. Everything that follows is true. Some will be hard to believe. I have many "former" fishing and hunting buddies that can verify most of it. (Former as in their wives won't let them go with Terry anymore.) The ones that still participate with me on fishing experiences must sign a release. I don't want to feel responsible for anything that might happen to them.

For years now, my wife has a saying she shouts at me occasionally: "The adventure continues." I can only hope so! She informed me that she has decided what my tombstone will say: "He had more fun than anybody." Well, it's true, and I hope that continues. Remember, life's not fun if you're not having fun. As of January 2016, she increased my life insurance policy. She added a one-hundred-thousand-dollar payment for "accidental death away from work." She claims she has already won the lottery, just hasn't been paid yet. I can't blame her for playing the odds. Our daughters came up with a nickname just to make fun of me as I was always telling them some of these stories during their growing-up years. They'd say, "Dad, you were Maximum Teenager." Yes, I was.

Now come with me—up McHenry Creek without a paddle.

If you never did you should. These things are fun, and fun is good. —Dr. Seuss

---

Chapter 1

"The Beans Always Come Up"

(Karma)

There is an old story of a father teaching his son a lesson about life. The story takes place back in the 1950s. There was a creek near their home, and it was the son's custom to go fishing with his buddies every Saturday during the spring. They would grab their poles as soon as their moms would let them away after breakfast. This particular morning, the father wanted his son to help him with their garden. They planted quite a crop of fresh vegetables that they would enjoy for months. The son was now old enough to help his dad, and good old dad wanted him to help out with some of the chores. The son was devastated that he could not go fishing with his friends. His dad informed him that he could go, but he would have to plant the green beans while the dad was on the other side of the garden planting his tomatoes and potatoes.

Dad had showed him how to make a row in the dirt, drop in the seeds, and cover them up just right. He was doing just fine but noticed there were a lot of seeds. He remembered that Dad had told him, "As soon as you finish all the seeds, you can go fishing." Suddenly, an idea formed in his young brain. If I just sling these seeds across this end of the garden, they will all be gone. So, he did just that. He went to the other end of the garden where Dad was and showed him the empty bucket. Dad thanked him for helping and told him he could go.

A couple of weeks went by, and one Saturday morning at breakfast, the dad asked the son to walk with him out to the garden and let him show the son all the vegetables that were starting to sprout. They started at the end where Dad had planted and worked their way to the other side. When they got to the area where the beans had been planted, they could see where a couple of rows of beans were popping up through the soil, and suddenly, beans were coming up all over the place. It was obvious what had happened. The father turned to his son and said, "Always remember, son, in life, the beans will always come up."

One afternoon back in about 1977 or 1978, one of my fishing buddies and I hooked up my boat and headed to a large creek with an area you could barely launch your boat. You couldn't back in too far or you might get stuck. We saw some buckets near the launch, and being nosy, we looked around. There were small perch and tadpoles that you could use for baiting trotlines or yo-yos in the buckets. There was no one around, and we had a few yo-yos with us, so we took the buckets. I backed in the trailer, and my friend cranked it up and pulled the boat off the trailer. I pulled the truck away and parked it and ran to the boat and jumped in. We were fishing some spinner baits in a lot of brush along the bank and setting a few yo-yos. We noticed someone had tied on many limb lines baited with live perch and tadpoles. We made fun of the guy as he didn't really know how to fish. About a half mile from where we started, I noticed up ahead one of the limb lines had a fish. As we got closer, I could tell it was a pretty good flathead catfish. Turned out he weighed about seven to eight pounds. We discussed our options and decided that the lines were abandoned, and the fish would die if we didn't take it off, and so we put it in our live well. We caught a few bass to go with our big cat, and it was getting late. We headed for the truck.

When fishing buddy ran the boat up to the bank, and I had jumped off to back in the trailer, we noticed another truck there. Turns out the fellow with the limb lines had launched after we had started fishing. We had a confrontation with him later on where he accused us of stealing his flathead. We foolishly admitted to catching the fish on a spinner bait. He assured us he knew more about cat fishing than anyone, and flatheads would only be caught on perch or tadpoles. An argument ensued, and he finally relented knowing he could not prove it. He informed us that we might have gotten away with his big fish, but he knew that we knew we were lying. He made some smart-aleck remark about "hoping we choked on it" and got in his boat and motored away.

Anyway, I backed the trailer in the creek. My buddy started running the boat up on the trailer. I saw in the mirror that he was not able to get the boat all the way up on the trailer, so I decided to back in a little farther. Suddenly, my back tires dropped about a foot straight down. The bank had a drop-off, and we were stuck! We tried everything, but the truck would not pull out. We looked at the other truck, and the keys were in it, and he had a chain. (Hey, it was his fault leaving his keys. What a moron.) We started the truck and backed it up to ours. We tried as hard as we could but could not pull it out. We were spinning all over the place and probably overheating the guy's truck and probably burned up his clutch. Little did we know, we would run into the guy later. We finally gave up and walked up to the highway, and we headed for the nearest house. An older lady lived there and was very reluctant to allow us in to call for a wrecker. We attempted to convince her we were not ordinary criminals, and just because we were all muddy and haggard looking, it would be okay to let us in. She did not agree and locked us out of her house, but she did make the call to the wrecker service. We walked back to the truck and waited. By now, other trucks were there to launch. We had everyone blocked. The guy whose fish we "rescued" and whose truck we "borrowed" had come back and offered to help. We thanked him but turned him down since we knew it wouldn't work from trying it earlier. We even wondered why he would offer to help us, knowing we had taken his fish. We decided that God must have spoken to him about helping those that can't take care of themselves or something. The wrecker finally came and pulled us out.

So although we didn't choke on the fish, we "borrowed" his bait, "rescued" his fish, used his truck without permission, scared an old lady, and made a bunch of people mad that couldn't get their boats launched. Of course, we got stuck and had to pay a wrecker.

Like the man said, your beans will always come up!

Chapter 2

"Has This Motor Been Underwater?"

Great things are done by a series of small things

brought together. —Vincent Van Gogh

a) Great things are done:

Catching a lot of big fish

b) By a series of small things:

Rods and reels, check

Spinner baits and plastic worms, check

Boat and trailer, check

Gas for motor, check

Battery charged, check

Trolling motor and paddle, check

Tighten motor to boat—oops!

Yes, we've lost the motor off the back of our boat many times. The guys I've always fished with and I are like kids at Christmas when it comes to going fishing. Can't sleep the night before and forget things due to being in a hurry. Sometimes those overlooked details can devastate a potentially great day.

We've done a vast portion of our fishing in oxbow lakes just off the many rivers in Arkansas. Swamps, sloughs, snaky little potholes, anywhere that might hold some fish. Sometimes they are very hard to get into. You may have to drag your small flat-bottom through the woods. In the late 1980s, I even built an axle with motorcycle wheels that fit over the top of my boat so that when you got to the place on the river where the oxbow is located, you set the wheels on the bank, take the motor and gas tank out of the boat, and drag the boat up on the axle and roll it through the woods to the small lake. Just whatever we could do to get to a fishing hole that not many would attempt. It takes a lot of concentration to remember all the little things while going from river to lake, lake to river, and such. For some reason, tightening the motor back onto the boat was the one little detail we seemed to forget the most.

1. Meet the Mechanic

One afternoon, one of our fishing buddies and my brother lost their motor (a borrowed motor) at an oxbow lake in east Arkansas. Someone never tightened it up before they left the launch area. They were motoring down the shallow lake and hit a stump just under the water. The motor jumped straight up and off the back of the boat, pulled the gas line loose, and settled on the bottom about four feet deep, still running till it choked out (drowned). Submerged motors are easy to find; just look for the fuel bubbling to the surface. A motor taking that kind of abuse will have to spend a few days in the shop under the care of a top-notch mechanic, getting cleaned out and tuned back up before putting it back into use. In other words, it ruins fishing for a few days.

2. Trolls

I took a young fellow fishing at Maddox Bay one Saturday in 1992. He informed me he had never been fishing. I should have directed him to someone who was luckier than me while on a fishing adventure, but I thought, surely I can get him home all safe and sound without any tragic consequences. He knew nothing of preparation, so I did all the work myself. Just before launching, I took the motor out of the truck and set it on the back of the boat. I don't know what happened next, but I never tightened the motor to the boat. I hooked up the gas line, told him to climb into the operator's seat, and showed him how to crank it up. I backed the trailer down the launch ramp with him in the seat. When the boat floated off the trailer, I pulled up the hill to the parking area. I was walking back down to the shoreline watching him pulling the cord until the motor started. He was having a little fun motoring around killing time while I approached. He suddenly turned the motor sharp toward me and gave it full throttle. The torque on the motor caused it to jump straight up and off the boat. It was going full blast, and I can still see the motor breaking the fuel line and traveling about five feet before it sank. I was truly impressed that the motor could travel that far before sinking. The water was six feet deep. I scanned for the sheen of fuel on the water surface and then tiptoed around the area until I found the motor with my feet and went down and pulled it over to the bank. We loaded up and headed for home. Another fishing trip down the drain, literally.

A few days later when I picked up the motor from the shop, the mechanic asked me if the motor had been underwater. I informed him that the motor had been stolen by the troll that lives under the bridge crossing McHenry Creek and I wasn't sure what all he had done to it before I recovered it.

3. Gypsies

On another trip to Round Pond with my brother's boat and motor, we were slowly motoring up a slough full of stumps. Of course, we hit one.

Fishing buddy: "ahhhh!"

Me (turning and looking toward the back of the boat): "nooooo! Not again!"

Fishing buddy: "I can't hold it."

Me: "Don't let go."

Fishing buddy: "Help!"

Me: "Rats."

Me: "It's only a few feet deep. I think it's my turn to go in and get it."

Fishing buddy: "Don't tell your brother."

Meanwhile, next day.

Mechanic: "Has this motor been underwater?"

Me: "You know, I'm not sure. Some Gypsies took it, and I just got it back."

4. Bigfoot

Motor loose. I hit stump. Motor hops up and off the boat. Motor does all it can to keep running and stay above water but sinks after a run of about four feet. Fortunately, we do most of our fishing in small boats with small motors in shallow water. Again, I look for the fuel surfacing and go over the side to retrieve the motor. Drive to shop.

Mechanic: "Has this motor been underwater?"

Me: "Have you ever heard of bigfoot?"

The advantage of a bad memory is that one enjoys several times the same good things for the first time. — Friedrich Nietzsche

[Or in my case, the stupid things.]

Chapter 3

The Trouble with Boat Trailers

Be Prepared. --the Boy Scouts motto

In reality, a fellow ought to be able to fish all his life and not worry about his boat trailer. But that would take some effort like preventive maintenance on the trailer. You know, stuff like packing the bearings regularly, checking the leaf springs to make sure there are no cracks, making sure the hitch is fastened to the truck correctly. I think it's called "the little things."

Looking back, I have not been very prepared when it comes to my boat trailer. I have had many mishaps over the years. I wish I could give a quality reason for this, but it is simply due to the fact that I just get all excited about fishing and don't think of things that should be taken more seriously. I'm certain most of you that are reading this would not make these mistakes, but surely, I'm not the only one that is this lazy.

1970s

Back in the late 1970s, we fished in a small lake in northern Saline County. It had small cottages and cabins built all around the shoreline, and therefore, many boat docks for bass habitat. Most of the fish were small, but we could catch seventy to one hundred in about a half day fishing. Have done it several times. The problem was that the old county road out there was in terrible condition. Potholes everywhere. It was a rough ride pulling a boat. At the time, I had a big and heavy fifteen-and-a-half-foot long aluminum boat with a forty horsepower Evinrude. The motor was 1960s vintage, and that meant it was big and heavy too. A fellow had to drive very slowly on such roads. The boat was loaded on a secondhand trailer that was purchased cheap without an inspection of the wear and tear. When you get one this cheap, you shouldn't expect much, I guess.

My friend and I were on the return trip after just smoking the bass at the lake. We were about halfway back to Pulaski County when a sudden bump or something took place. I started slowing down and carefully applying the brake in order not to jackknife the trailer. The leaf spring had broken on the right side. The trailer bounced and dropped. The axle was now pointing backward and causing the trailer to be high on the left side. This caused the boat to lunge hard to the right and brake off the upright on the trailer. The boat was still hooked to the front of the trailer, so the boat and trailer were spread in a V-shape following my truck. I didn't drag it far, but it had already worn a hole in the aluminum boat on the bottom of the right side.

I had to leave the boat and trailer on the side of the road and head to a friend's house to get another trailer and make our way back out there to retrieve my boat. We took both trucks and a chain, so we could line the trucks up, his in front of mine, and drag the boat onto the new trailer attached to my truck. The boat would be easy to patch. The trailer, I took the wheels and the winch assembly off and just left the frame in the ditch. I am certain that it was salvaged as scrap metal the next day.

1980s

Somewhere about 1983, we were traveling to another lake in Saline County to load up on some more bass. There was only one launch ramp on the lake, and it was on the far west side. Most folks would not go there due to the rough and rocky road. Roads like that are tough on boats and trailers. We like to go where others won't. When you finally get there, you turn onto a still rougher section of the road that leads to the lake. Literally, boulders are driven over or, hopefully, around. I was just creeping along when the springs broke off on the right side. Since the springs are the only thing that holds the axle to the frame, the axle was now pointing almost straight backward. The boat had now fallen off the right side of the trailer. You know, the famous V-shape since the boat was still attached to the front of the trailer. We spent about thirty minutes removing the 9.9 horsepower motor from the back of the boat and pulling the boat backward off the trailer and out of the way.

We began trying to push the axle back under the trailer. We would get a big rock and put it under and behind the right side of the trailer to block it and back the truck up thus putting pressure against the axle, and finally, after a few attempts, we had it almost lined back up under the trailer. There was a stump of an old tree right behind us and just off the road. I maneuvered the trailer axle up against the stump and backed into it until my axle was lined perfectly. "Now what?" my buddy asked.

"We don't have extra springs." I assured him that, indeed, there was more than one way to skin a cat (an old saying—I don't who said it or what they were really referring to). I took a medium-sized rope from the bed of the truck and tied it around the frame and axle. I wrapped it around very tightly and began to use an entire roll of duct tape, wrapping it around and around the axle and frame, thus securing everything in place.

We stood back and smiled at our accomplishment. My friend informed me he was sure it wouldn't work, but I sured him right back that the fishing gods had never broken my trailer more than once on any single trip. And since I was so sure, we went on and launched the boat and fished all afternoon and simply forgot about it until we headed to the shore about dark. I expertly backed the crippled trailer into the water and loaded the boat back on and secured it. As we started down the road, my friend alerted me to something: "It's doubtful that we make it," and "We're out of duct tape!" The duct tape comment did send a chill down my spine, so I told him he was probably right, but I wasn't planning on staying the night there. So on we went. I drove extremely slow, and it took almost two hours to drive the thirty-eight miles home.

New Boy Scouts motto: Duct tape, don't leave home without it!

1990s

It takes about an hour to prop up a trailer and pull the wheels in order to grease both sets of bearings. It is something that is recommended by anyone who knows wheels and bearings. I usually remember about every other year or four. It works most of the time.

We had been fishing all day at a lake in east Arkansas. It was close to sundown when we decided to load up and head for home. We had driven about sixteen miles back to I-40 when I noticed smoke coming from the right side of my trailer. "Burned up another bearing," I whimpered. I pulled over just short of the interstate on the access road. We disconnected the trailer and dragged the boat up into my full size, eight-foot bed of the truck, nine and a half feet with the tailgate down. We loaded everything back up and removed the wheels and winch assembly from the trailer and left a note on the frame—in case a state trooper came by—informing them that I would be back the next morning to recover my trailer.

So next morning, I borrowed an empty trailer and took another friend to go get my trailer. By the time we got there, I noticed it had become someone else's trailer due to the fact that it was not where I left it. Oh well, another life lesson that I didn't understand. You would think that some of these so-called lessons would take hold, but looking back, I don't think they ever did.

The 2000s

Yes, it happened again, but it's starting to get stupid, so I'm going to keep the rest to myself; but this time, it was the left side spring that broke, so the famous V-shape had the boat dragging on the other side.

The 2016

Can you believe it, the axle on my trailer is bent right now!

By seeking and blundering, we learn. --Johann Wolfgang von Goethe (No, that doesn't fit.)

Failure is instructive. The person who really thinks learns quite as much from his failures as from his successes. -- John Dewey) (Nope.)

In the arena of life, so many lessons are taught, but few are taken, and few are applied. --Ernest Agyemang Yeboah). (This guy must have heard about me.)

Chapter 4

The Art of Sculling (Paddling)

Life is hard. It's even harder if you're stupid. —John Wayne

Just curious, what do you use for a paddle when you need one? Most would use, uh, a paddle? What if you don't have one? I remember several hunting or fishing trips that turned into an adventure simply by forgetting to bring along a paddle. It's called not being prepared. Or as Big John put it...

I am very skilled at sculling a boat. I can keep it straight and gradually move it down the shoreline as my partner and I fire our spinner baits or jigs along the brush and logs. I'm old enough to have been there and done that before we ever had electric motors for such labor. It is a forgotten art. But if you fish some of the places we do, you can't carry a battery or electric motor through the woods to a boat that is tied up at another oxbow.

Duck hunters and PJs (perch jerkers) would leave boats tied up at these hard-to-get-to lakes. In the eighties, they were tied with ropes. In the nineties, they started using chains and locks. So I had a backpack I carried with me. The contents were as follows: hacksaw, pliers, wrenches, several new locks, small set of bolt cutters. We would simply get the chain undone somehow and add our own lock to the chain. Sometimes there would be as many as a dozen locks on the chain—several people made their own access to the boat. There would always be a boat we could use, so you simply carry a small sculling paddle.

All that's fine and dandy, but what about the other times when something goes haywire, and you need a paddle or something to propel the boat when you are not planning on sculling? It would be nice to remember to bring along a paddle, or some other device that can be substituted for a paddle. Anything. A flat board, a hubcap, a push pole—anything. Let's see how cunning and resourceful the McHenry Creek boys can be.

Who was supposed to get the paddle?

Sometime back in the seventies: "Who was supposed to get the paddle?" There's never been a more irrelevant question ever asked.

My friend, his brother, and I had decided to take our bows and head to a lake that has a few islands that deer inhabit. It's easy; you drop two hunters off on the lake side of the island, and the guy in the boat motors quickly to the side of the island closest to the main shore. The two then spread out and sneak to the other side. If there are any deer on the island, they will head for shore. The guy in the boat then herds them back onto the island with the boat. The great hunters proceed to shoot at the deer with arrows. It's exciting. It might be cheating, but I'm not sure the game warden was aware of this type of hunting. Anyway, it was back in the early seventies, and I'm not sure they had rules about it. (Knowing us, we would have ignored them anyway.)

It was pretty cold and windy; twenty-eight degrees and a twenty-mile-per-hour wind from the west. I had borrowed a boat larger than what we had from my uncle. An old Razorback ski boat from the sixties. No seats, just an open slanted bottom. We jumped in and took off for the island to the east. Of course, there were no paddles or trolling motor. We didn't need them anyway. My friend dropped his brother and me off at the west end of the island, and he headed around to get ready. A large doe had already took to the water by the time he got there. He chased her back onto the island where his brother and I were ready with bows drawn. We let fly and both missed. We jumped up and took off after her while fitting another arrow. We stopped about halfway across the island and waited. She would have to come back by one of us. After several minutes, my buddy started hollering at us, "Did you get it? Where are you?" Brother and I started making our way to the far end. No deer. We couldn't figure out what happened to her. Fishing buddy finally motored up to our end, and we were just standing there arguing about who let the deer get away and wondering where "away" was. Suddenly, brother hollered, "There it is!" She had taken to the big water side of the island and was almost to the bank over three hundred yards away.

By now, we were cold and had given up and decided to head back. It was several miles back into that freezing wind. The strong wind was "whitecapping" and causing the waves to splash over the front of the boat. The bottom of the boat had become a sheet of ice. We were covered in ice. Fishing buddy was in the only seat, steering the boat. Brother and I were slip-sliding all over the icy hull. About a quarter of a mile from the ramp, the motor started sputtering and ran out of gas. And there we were. Our ice boat was being blown the wrong direction by a freezing wind.

We scrounged in the boat and came up with the only thing that could be used as a paddle. For some reason, there was a hubcap off an old car under the console for the steering wheel. I lay across the front hull of the icy boat and began to pull that hubcap through the water to get us to the bank. My two companions were holding my legs to keep from sliding into the freezing water. Man, it was cold! Paddling with a hubcap. I wonder if Big John had heard about us.

Oh yeah, the irrelevant question. When fishing buddy screamed, "Who was supposed to get a paddle?" Brother responded, "*$@# the paddle! Who was supposed to get some gas?"

Paddling with a two-by-four?

My friend and I were heading to a private reservoir we had permission to fish in. That's right, we weren't sneaking in this time. It was loaded with big bass. We had caught several over six pounds and a couple over seven. Actually, we had previously caught one that might have weighed seven. We backed up to the edge of the water and pushed the boat in. We grabbed our fishing rods and were fixing to shove off when we realized we had forgotten the electric motor. Battery, but no trolling motor. We did the usual debate about whose fault it was, but the fact remained, we had nothing to propel the boat. I asked, "When are we going to remember to always put a paddle in the boat?" We determined that the answer was probably never. We scrounged around the area that the farmer stored his tools and found a short two-by-four. I informed fishing buddy that I could do it but would probably get tired and have to rest. We fished for a little while, but it was just too difficult. We had a friend that managed a sporting goods store in Little Rock. We knew one of his employees' grandmother lived in the nearby city. We drove to a store and called him. He called us back and gave us the address to the grandmother's. The employee kept fishing stuff at his grandmother's, and yes, there was a trolling motor there. The fishing trip was saved after a two-hour delay. I'm sure there is a moral to this story and this kind of behavior, but we were just too stupid to figure it out.

B*lah-blah, blah-blah, blah-blah.* —John Wayne

Chapter 5

Terry the Safety Guy

Stupid is as Stupid does. —F. Gump

I've been a private OSHA consultant for eighteen years. Most of my workdays are spent instructing a break room full of workers on various safety topics. I am a HAZMAT specialist and instructor. I am also well versed in the Confined Space Entry and Rescue guidelines. I teach these topics all over the country. I am known as the "safety guy" by thousands of workers. This morning, I was thinking, how can OSHA safety apply to my fishing hobby?

See if you can relate to some of them.

1. I have fallen asleep in my deer stand many times. I have fallen out of that widow-maker multiple times. Some of the falls were due to being a sleepyhead, and some from the stand being constructed poorly. I remember in 1976, after regaining my senses from landing about twelve feet on the ground below my stand, thinking, This is stupid. I should get a rope or something and tie myself to the tree. So I did from then on. (Yes, I invented the tree stand safety strap the next year.)

Incident: Fall from stand and land on ground.

OSHA-recommended prevention: (a) hunt from ground, (b) stop building poorly constructed homemade stands, or (c) tie yourself to the tree.

2. I have fallen out of a boat eleven times. A few were in cold weather on hunting trips. Most were fishing adventures.

Incident: Fall from boat while fishing.

OSHA-recommended prevention: Fish from bank (if continue to fish from boat, a dependable floatation device is advised).

3. I have climbed over fences hundreds of times while hunting or fishing. Sometimes it was okay, most times it was not. Fences are there for a reason. Either to keep cattle in or keep unwanted people out—or both. I along with some of my friends have been arrested twice for trespassing while on hunting trips, simply because we were caught on the wrong side of the fence. Both took place in the mid-1970s. (Why does young and stupid continue to be an excuse?)

If you are not extremely careful, you can hurt yourself climbing over or through fences. On one occasion, I cut myself pretty badly on barbed wire. I knew a teenager that shot himself in the shoulder while going through the wire. (Yes, he did it in the seventies.)

Incident: Injured while climbing over or through fences.

OSHA-recommended prevention: (a) use gate, (b) carry wire cutters, or (c) get rid of guns and fishing poles, thus eliminating the need to cross the fence.

4. I have killed many deer. Most were legal. The problem with shooting a deer is that now you have to drag it for some distance to get to your truck. After about twenty years of dragging, we built a two-wheel cart to slide the deer on and now roll it to truck. Before we became smart, you could easily hurt your back dragging a big, heavy deer. I have killed deer that weighed over two hundred pounds after field dressing. (Not many, but still, a few. Okay, only one that was that big.) Usually, a field-dressed buck still weighs from 140 to 160 pounds. Bottom line, dragging a deer is not ergonomically sound.

Incident: Pulled muscle in back while dragging deer to truck.

OSHA-recommended prevention: hunt from truck.

5. I have had to spend the night in jail only one time in my entire life. November of 1975. It broke me from going to jail. Terrible place. County lockup in some small dreary little town. We had been spotlighting deer. During the search and seizure, they discovered a few "other" things that we had done. My so-called buddies had some whacky tobacky hidden in their car. I knew better than to be involved with that sort of thing. I avoided any kind of doping. It's just stupid, and most people know it. But I knew they partook of such things, and my mother had warned me about hanging out with guys that did these types of things. But they had been spotlighting all week, and it got me excited to go with them Wednesday night. They were telling me all the deer they were seeing. I thought, Just this once. (Yeah, that

makes it okay.)

Incident: Arrested for being involved in illegal activities.

OSHA-recommended prevention: (a) honor you mother and father (b) take your own truck. (You know, the truck without any weed hidden in it.)

6. I remember the day I first tried using what were called "phones" to shock fish. It was some silly looking little cranking device. It was like an old phone you would see in a 1950s movie. That might have been what it was. You cranked the little handle on the side to energize the phone, therefore getting the operator. But we weren't calling anyone. We would stretch a wire across a pond and connect one end of the wire to the phone. It had some kind of winding inside that would generate a little bit of electricity as you cranked it, therefore stunning the fish, and then we would gather them up. (Well, that was what we had heard.) Again, we were young and stupid; and after about an hour of continually shocking ourselves, we surrendered and threw the whole gizmo in the pond.

Incident: Shock oneself while conducting illegal activities.

OSHA-recommended prevention: (a) wear personal protective equipment like rubber gloves and boots, (b) use a qualified electrician, (c) stop being stupid.

7. Have you ever, or how many times have you hooked yourself or your buddy? Ouch! When that hook gets

past the barb, it is painful and nasty. Although not near as painful and nasty as attempting to get unhooked. This can range from attempting to jiggle it out (more ouch), or curling the hook that is stuck in your body until the point comes out of a new hole in your skin, then cutting the barb off with wire cutters and pulling it back out the original hole. I cringed as I watched a friend do this one day while we were snagging carp below a spillway. A fish he had hooked and pulled from the water slipped from his hands and returned the favor by slamming the giant snagging hook deep into the thigh of his right leg. It flounced once and shook free from the hook and went back into the water.

Or that stupid thing about wrapping fishing line around the hook many times and yanking. If you attempt that one, try being the one doing the yanking and not the one with the hook stuck in you past the barb.

Then, of course, there is going to the ER, but where is the adventure in that? And it takes too long, and we don't want to waste any more fishing time than what is absolutely necessary. I have been fishing with guys that were forced to fish most of the day with a hook or lure hanging from their head after being hooked.

Incident: Hooking your buddy while fishing.

OSHA-recommended prevention: (a) place a bottle of hydrogen peroxide in boat, or (b) fish alone (at least this lowers the odds of someone getting hooked).

8. I've been lost many times. I have spent the night in

strange places three times from being lost. I used to wonder why all the compasses I've ever purchased did not work. I wonder what OSHA would have to say about a guy like me?

Incident: Getting lost in woods or river.

OSHA-recommended prevention: (a) take a course on compass reading, (b) stop hunting and fishing and stay home with wife, or (c) hunt and fish in backyard.

9. OSHA tells us that the most common injury comes from slips, trips, and falls from the same level. I'm not sure where to start with this one. Maybe I should write an entire chapter on this topic. Let's start with the snakebite.

Incident: Slipped on slick rock and fell on snake.

OSHA-recommended prevention: (a) avoid stepping on slick rocks and (b) pay attention to where you are walking so you will recognize oncoming hazards (you know, like a big ugly cottonmouth coiled up, ready to strike.)

10. Another slip or trip and fall: early January 2016. (It's still happening.) These days, I fish alone most of the time (duh). I had just backed the trailer in and pulled the boat off and beached it beside the ramp. I then jumped out and pulled the truck and trailer into a parking spot. I had already installed the front pedestal for the front seat but not put the seat on yet. I was stepping into the front of boat and pushing with the

other foot in order to float away from the bank. I somehow stumbled (imagine that) and was falling face-first onto the front deck. The aluminum pedestal was approaching my right eye at a great rate of speed. I thrust my right arm to block the metal spike from forcing the lens of my glasses deep into my brain. I struck it hard. Now my right arm just above the wrist is in much pain. I headed back to the truck to get my first aid kit and patch myself up in order to get to fishing. I always carry a trusty bandanna or two. I pulled the one from my back pocket, folded it nicely, and wrapped it around my right arm. I reached under the seat and found my first aid kit. I wrapped a couple of layers of duct tape around the bandanna pretty tight. Ahh! As good as new.

I successfully pushed the boat from the bank this time and jumped in. I motored about fifteen minutes to one of my favorite spots and started attempting to outsmart some fish. I got to noticing the pain in my right arm was not subsiding. As a matter of fact, I began to realize it was worse. I gave up after about an hour. I spent the next forty-five minutes getting the boat back onto the trailer with a broken arm. (That's superhero stuff.) I drove home and iced my arm. Monday morning, my doc informed me it was a hairline fracture of the radius. I was not sure what that meant, I just knew it was hurting and had ruined my fishing trip. I had to wear a brace for a few weeks.

Incident: Fall into boat.

OSHA-recommended prevention: (a) stay out of boat, (b)

sell haunted boat, or (c) take up fishing from bank.

11. Another slip, trip, and fall. Somewhere and sometime in the eighties, we were again launching in an old river lake. We had a small oxbow in mind that we figured not many folks had fished recently due to the fact it was hard to get into. The water level had just dropped another foot in the last eight hours, making it difficult to get into some of the lakes, but again, but we had our ways. The two-by-twelve-foot board leading from the bank to the dock had been just under the water line. This causes it to gather mud, slime, moss, and other slippery things. Now it is just above the waterline and still damp. Of course, we were in a hurry to get going, and the condition of the walkway did not figure in our thought process. I had just parked the truck after launching the boat with my partner aboard, and he had pulled over to the dock and tied up to wait for me. I was trotting down the hill as quickly as possible, and just as my first foot hit the plank, I was airborne. Any and every Olympic diver wishes they had this film footage. I'm pretty sure I set some record of how many twists you can make while being such a short distance from the water. What they can do from ten meters can actually be done from zero meters by a master slip slider like myself. After two full flips and four and a half twists, I landed square on the board where it attaches to the dock. I think it's called "sticking the landing."

Exactly where my left side struck the board was now in much pain. I struggled to catch my breath. I attempted to communicate with my fishing buddy that I was in trouble while he yelled at me to stop horsing around and hurry up. After he finally realized that I had "done it again," he decided to exit the boat and check on me. It took about thirty minutes to regain partial cognitive skills and stand.

I was having a little trouble breathing, but I was sure it would get better soon. He informed me that the pain in my side was also temporary. We were soon motoring down the bay, but the pain was still lingering. Fishing trip did not last long as I soon realized I needed more medical attention than he was offering.

The next day, I discovered that there is nothing the doctor can do with three broken ribs but offer pain medicine and advice. I accepted the pain pills and left his office. As I pulled away from his parking area, I remember telling myself I needed to find a better doctor. I later learned during another visit to his office for help, that with me in mind, he was thinking he needed better quality patients. Although he told me he appreciated all the insurance claims he had made on my behalf.

Incident: Slip on slick board while rushing to boat.

OSHA-recommended prevention: (a) calm down and slow down—attempting to arrive a couple of minutes quicker really won't allow you to catch any more fish; (b) stop purchasing fishing license, thus avoiding the need to hurry to boat, or (c) conduct all fishing activities from the bridge that crosses McHenry Creek.

"A prudent man foresees the difficulties ahead and

prepares for them; the simpleton goes blindly on and suffers the consequences" (Proverbs 22:3).

Well, that proves it. God does know the future. That verse was written thousands of years before I was born.

Chapter 6

Dear Diary: Let's Go Fishing

Murphy's Law: If it can go wrong, it will go wrong.

God: The earth is cursed.

After about a million fishing trips and encountering two million zany happenstances, I have become a believer in the fact that there is something out there greater than puny humans. You just can't have this many weird, unfortunate adventures by accident. It might be called Murphy. I have heard a lot about him and have been fighting this guy most of my life. But I cannot believe that it's that simple, that some guy named Murphy is out to get me. I believe it might be a higher power. The Bible calls it pestilence. "The earth is cursed," the Bible says. I believe it, I guess I have my whole life. Ever since Adam followed his wife's advice, a whole lot of things have been going wrong. Weeds now grow in gardens. You step on a sticker every time you go barefoot. It gets cold in the winter. Sometimes it doesn't rain for months. The sun is always in your eyes. You're running late, and someone's grandmother just pulled out in front of you. The toll booth says "exact change only." The wind always blows hard when you go fishing. Add your own. It's a combination of Murphy and pestilence. The earth, sure enough, is cursed, and as long as people like us are involved, there are going to be some strange happenings.

Most folks just call it Murphy's Law. But I know better.

It's the pestilence the Bible spoke of. It doesn't have to be drought or raining frogs or locusts. It's all the little things in your life that you can't explain, but they just keep happening. It's like working on your truck, and just when your hands get all greasy and oily, your nose itches and you have to go to the bathroom. If you drop something, it will always roll to the least accessible place on the floor. Just when you get into the shower, the phone rings. You can name thousands. People say, "Old Murphy, he's always watching." I just can't buy solely into this phenomenon. There must be a higher power directing all these coincidences. But it's something. It's either Murphy or pestilence or both. Maybe that's why you hear, "Life is hard and then you die." Can't argue with that.

I urge you to start paying attention to all the little things out there that happen to you constantly. Whatever it is, it's real. It just happens to some people more than others. You know, me.

Let's go fishing.

I actually was the principal of a school in a former life. Small private school. The principal was also the janitor, the nurse maid, the hall monitor, vomit mopper during stomach virus season, and in the summer, the contractor for all the remodeling that takes place. A very busy job. About the only vacation I got for three years was spring break. I just told them to find a way to do without me for this one week of the year.

Spring break 1991. Fishing buddy and I were going on a

weeklong fishing trip. I was hoping that Murphy would not go with us this time.

Dear Diary:

Monday morning

So far, the only thing going wrong was a headache that wouldn't go away. After loading everything and checking it twice, we pulled out of the driveway. We were pulling his pop-up camper. We had the flat-bottom boat tied on top of the camper. We hadn't gone a mile when the camper started weaving a little in the rearview mirror. I pulled over, and one of the trailer tires was flat. Something was telling me that we should turn back while we were still this close to home, but we did not. So we changed the tire and continued on, now without a spare. Gutsy. I remembered a phone call that I must place, so we stopped at a pay phone. What I thought would take a couple of minutes had now lasted fifteen minutes. Delayed again. I remember wondering if the entire trip would be like this.

Dear Diary:

Monday midday

After about a two-hour journey, we arrived at our campsite. After we got everything unloaded and set up, we moved over to the launch ramp and put the boat in. I was going to crank up the 9.9 Evinrude and idle over to where we would keep our boat tied up just below our camper. My motor would not start. It was a great motor.

A one cranker. But I could not get it started. So, we backed the truck back down to the water and pulled the motor from the boat and put it into the bed of the truck. There was a marine shop a few miles away. We took it to the mechanic, and he graciously loaned us a 9.9 Mercury to use until he fixed ours.

Dear Diary:

Monday afternoon

We put his motor on our boat, loaded all our gear, and were going to motor over to a spot we had been told was a very good area for bass fishing. The mechanic's motor would not start. Murphy is smiling. Fishing buddy mumbles about why we didn't go home after the flat. My head was still hurting.

We used our trolling motor to fish till sundown. We caught a few small bass. "Let's just go fix supper," I told fishing buddy. "Good enough," he replied. On the way to the lake, we had stopped at a grocery store to pick up our supplies for the week. We picked out a couple of steaks to grill the first night. A properly grilled medium steak was sounding good. We tied up the boat, climbed up the bank, and started getting ready for supper.

Dear Diary:

Monday night

We attempted to light the stove in the camper. No luck. I asked fishing buddy if there was fuel in the propane tank. He offered a puzzled look. There was not. It was now raining. We couldn't even build a fire to cook the steaks. We decided we would get the tank filled tomorrow and just "wing it" for supper tonight. I was watching fishing buddy as he ate Vienna sausages and some chips. I was eating directly from a can of Ranch Style Beans. Gross. I remember hoping the headache go away before morning.

Dear Diary:

Tuesday morning

Why does this camper smell like a portable toilet at a construction site? Dang that fishing buddy and his eating habits! I'll take it up with him later. We enjoyed a lovely breakfast consisting of marked-down, day-old Hostess cupcakes. Anything to try to get over the night before. The rain had stopped but was supposed to start back on Wednesday. We decided this would be a good day to drive the thirty miles and play golf at what was supposed to be a nice golf course in a nearby town. We dropped off the borrowed motor hoping to get ours back. He informed us that he needed to order some parts for mine but would have his running by the time we got back Tuesday afternoon. We advised him that we were certain that something else will happen to foil his plans, but that he should try anyway.

We soon found out that the directions we were given to the golf course were poor. Took an extra hour to get there. A black cat ran across the road just as we were pulling into the clubhouse. We laughed.

Our golf game was terrible, 88 and 92. We blamed it on the course being too wet. Couldn't be that we were just very bad at golf. We had burgers at the turn from the clubhouse. They tasted dirty. I asked fishing buddy if we should tell them they should clean the grill occasionally. He said no, that would just make them angry at us, and we still had nine holes to play. He thought that at the worst, we would start feeling better in a few hours. They had cute names for all their food items. Some named after famous golfers. The Arnold Palmer, the Jack Nicklaus, and so on. Our burger was named "The Gut Bomb." What were we thinking? Now my head and my stomach hurt.

We finally finished playing golf and headed back to camp. We looked for the black cat at the end of the driveway but didn't see it this time. Didn't matter, the damage was done. We stopped at a convenience store on the way back to camp for Big Gulp-size Cokes. Fishing buddy didn't see me, but I also found a rabbit's foot key chain next to the counter and purchased it.

Dear Diary:

Tuesday evening

Our motor was still not fixed. We picked up the Mercury again (he "fixed" it) and drove to our camper. We were envisioning those tasty steaks. We traded for a full bottle of propane for the stove. Now we could prepare proper meals. At least the steaks smelled delicious. That was the good part. They must have been cut with a hatchet from an old milk cow. The tongue from a leather boot would have been easier to chew.

We gave up and went to bed. I found myself wishing the rain would intensify in order to drown out fishing buddy's snoring. At least my head and stomach felt better.

Dear Diary:

Wednesday morning

We finished off our morning cupcakes and pushed the boat into the water. It seemed the east wind had intensified. It was also raining again, so we were wet and cold. I stuck a hook into my finger while changing baits. It hurt. We struggled to catch some fish, but they weren't cooperating either. After a few hours, we headed back. The borrowed Mercury was sputtering again. We had to use the electric motor to finally make it back. I tossed the rabbit's foot into lake. I made sure fishing buddy didn't see me. I knew it wouldn't work.

Dear Diary:

Wednesday noon

We feasted on bologna sandwiches. Another form of gut bomb. My system might never recover from this trip. Why didn't fishing buddy get smoked turkey or ham? I'll have to remember to ask him later. By now, we were barely speaking.

Dear Diary:

Wednesday night

My brother and his friend showed up. They were planning on finishing our trip with us. We explained to them that we were pretty much finished already. We enjoyed a decent supper and went to bed. Now we had four guys sleeping in the camper. Well, three. I just lay there listening to them snore in unison. Again, I found myself wishing it would rain harder to help cover the snoring.

Dear Diary:

Thursday morning

It's raining harder. Why is it that only the bad things you hope for happen? We helped them launch in the rain and both boats set out. They were motoring, and we just started fishing from the ramp having no motor that runs. They caught six. We caught two. Won't be much of a fish fry. Maybe we will catch a few more this afternoon. If not, I'll peel a few extra potatoes.

Dear Diary:

Thursday afternoon

Uneventful. We experienced another poor catch and headed to camp. We made a quick shelter from plastic sheeting in order to cook our fish and fried potatoes. A big fish fry during a fishing trip is hard to beat, even in the rain.

Dear Diary:

Thursday night

Their snoring had lost its rhythm. Nothing worse than three guys snoring haphazardly. I thought to myself, I'll catch up on sleep over the weekend. I placed pieces of rolled-up paper towels in my ears.

Dear Diary:

Friday morning

We woke to pouring rain and a strong east wind. I informed everyone that I'd had it. I whined about all the work I could have done at the school if only we had surrendered Monday when we experienced the flat. They convinced me to try to catch some fish for a few more hours. I finally succumbed but insisted on looking for four-leaf clovers first. Fishing buddy tossed salt over his left shoulder. Neither worked.

We caught five bass in the next three hours. I was thinking of taking up cursing or just attempting to put a curse on my friends. I was not satisfied that they were as miserable as I was. So let's take inventory: wet, cold, still windy and rainy, no motor, and minimal fish. Why are we still here? I'm going to go home and find the guy that told me fishing was fun. I'll put a curse on him.

Dear Diary:

Friday noon

We started packing. Everything was wet and muddy. We headed for home. When we got to the highway, we remembered we had to stop and get my motor. Now we had to unpack most of our load and start all over packing. The mechanic was pissed and started cursing at me because I was getting my motor before he had fixed it. "I've got parts on the way!" he shouted. I reminded him that he had the motor since Monday and apparently didn't know what he was doing. No wonder he was cursing at me. And of course, the last of my dry clothes were now wet. My brother started laughing. Now we all were. We tried to convince ourselves that there was always next time. I felt relieved that I did not put a curse on anyone. And when I got home, I was going to get myself a balloon.

No one can be uncheered with a balloon. —Winnie the
        Pooh

Chapter 7

High Water, Small Boats

Sometimes the Water Rises Quickly

"The greatest accomplishment is not in never falling but in rising again after you fall" (Vince Lombardi). I think he stole it from Ralph Waldo Emerson.

Most folks that hunt and fish have witnessed suddenly rising water. They have seen water released below a dam or a big rain. Most of the time, these things happen gradually. But most have never seen a wall of water coming at you or a river so high it has whirlpools scattered across the surface from shore to shore. Yes, I have experienced both. In my lifelong endeavor to have fun, I have attempted some things that seem foolish now. Okay, they were also foolish back then.

Some of my buddies and I tried something different for a couple of years back in the day. We decided to purchase some fur-bearing-animal traps. In the fall and winter, you can get a few bucks for hides from raccoon, fox, and mink. Sounded easy. We purchased a couple of dozen traps and would set them out around ponds, lakes, and small streams. And, of course, we caught some. Here is what we caught in order of how many we caught: at number 5, zero mink and fox; number 4, skunks; number 3, raccoons; number 2, possums; and at number 1, dogs! It's why we gave up. We got tired of releasing dogs from the trap and being bitten a few times. Nothing worse than parking near the lake where our traps were set and hearing the howling of a dog in the direction of our trapline. We sucked at trapping fur-bearing animals. So we came up with a better idea. We would float in a small flat-bottom boat down a stream at night and spotlight minks and raccoons and shoot them with a .22 rifle. Sounded like fun and some easy money. We didn't even know we were doing anything wrong. It was fur-bearing season, so we didn't think it mattered how we took the animals. We found out a few years later on a raccoon hunting/spotlighting trip that any animal taken with the use of spotlights is illegal. You must have a dog treeing the animals in order to shoot them. That was costly. Good for the Game and Fish for their effort in stopping spotlighting. We matured and have no ill will now for the fines they hammered us with. They caught the bad guys. It worked. We're good guys now. (Most of the time.)

We had this idea of parking one truck about four miles downstream and then driving the four to five miles upstream and putting in the boat. We would then float downstream shining the banks until we reached the other truck. We would then drive back to the other truck and come home. Sounded like a great plan. We even came up with a ballpark figure on how much we would earn during this trip.

After parking the first truck and driving to the launch area, we put in our small, light, twelve-foot boat with a thirty-two-inch bottom and fourteen-inch-high sides. We were approximately six-one at 240 pounds and six-three at 195 pounds. Yeah, way too big for such a battleship as we were boarding. And that's if we remain very still.

But with greed as the motivating factor, we could not be concerned about the little things.

So, we climbed in with our six-volt light and rifle and pushed off. The current was just right. I used a paddle to keep us heading downstream while using the light, and my buddy had the .22 ready. After about an hour, we had seen one mink. Turned out they were way too energetic to get a clean shot. We were discussing the possibility that this was another in a long string of stupid ideas when we heard a dog bark just downstream from our present location. We started shining the light in his direction, and there he was. Some mixed-breed small dog but seemed very friendly. We discussed what we should do and came to the conclusion that he was not one of the many dogs we had caught in our traps and would not hold a grudge toward us, so we pulled the boat close to the shore, and he jumped in. After a few minutes of testing him to see if it was a trick to get into our boat and bite us, we concluded that he was just a friendly dog. So now with the added weight, we had about one-inch clearance on the side of our boat. I had to continually inform my partner to stop squirming around, so we won't tip the boat over.

About another hour had passed when we heard thunder quickly approaching. And then it started raining. It actually started just upstream from us, and it was pouring. Some folks would say it was raining cats and dogs. This would be incorrect. It was a toad strangler, and every country boy in seven states knows that a toad strangler is much worse than cats and dogs. No offence to our newfound friend. He began to whimper. He realized as we did that the sides of our boat were getting closer to the water surface with all the rain collecting in the bottom. I took the six-volt light apart and used the housing for a water bailer. It would hold about a pint at a time. So we were gaining speed, and the possibility of our boat dipping under was becoming more real. I yelled at my partner to dip faster but remain very still in the process. He was now bailing as I attempted to keep the boat straight. We were still gaining speed due to the fact that the stream was rising, which means more water was flowing downstream.

That's when it happened. The flood had started upstream from us, and it was raining faster than the water could flow. This built up a wall of water a few feet high, and it was gaining on us. We heard it before we saw it, having no light anymore. The boat rose up suddenly; I realized what was going on, and it was even more imperative that I kept the boat straight. If we got even the slightest bit off center, we were going over. We obviously did not know where we were from side to side in this raging river, but suddenly, we were on the left side. We hit a shallow spot, which was probably the actual shoreline that was now underwater. The boat got sideways, and over we went. It was only about one and a half feet deep, so we were rolling over, boat on top, us on top, and over and over. It fortunately washed us to the new shoreline, and we pulled the boat out of the water. It was a miracle we were both safe. During this circus act, we lost man's best friend. He abandoned us in our time of disaster. He must have determined that anywhere, even lost in the woods, was better than being on board with the Gump brothers. We hold no grudge since we are sure he was correct.

After much discussion, we decided our best course of action was to wait for the rain to stop and the river to slow down. When the water would slow down, the small river would recede to its banks, and we could push back in. It would be a little swifter than normal, but I knew I could hold it straight. The river would only be about forty yards wide at that point.

After about another hour, the rain had ceased, and the river dropped back into its banks, so off we went. That's when we realized a very thick heavy fog had set in. We were wet and cold, and now we couldn't see. We continued to drift slowly and aimlessly. We tried to keep close to the right side since that was where we had parked the other truck. We had no sense of time or distance and were discussing how far downstream we would have to travel if we missed the truck in this fog. We figured it was about four more miles to the next bridge crossing this river. We decided not to dwell on it. After a short silence, we were joking about the dog when suddenly, it sounded as if we were in a large barrel with an echo—or under a bridge. I pulled the boat hard to the right to get to the bank and climbed up. Sure enough, we were at the bridge where we had parked. What luck! (Or was it angels.) We tied the boat up and started the truck and turned on the heater full blast! Finally, warm again. We took off to the other truck as fast as we could and headed home.

Yeah, we left the boat. We decided it was just too small for us, and if we had recovered it, that would have meant dragging it straight up from the river to the level area where the truck was parked. Very steep. About sixteen to eighteen feet. We discussed it and decided to abandon it. We knew we would end up using it again to do something stupid that might not turn out so well.

But I do wonder about that dog sometimes. Hope he's doing okay.

(Let's see, that was about thirty years ago. Times seven for dog years. That means he would be about 210 years old. Yeah, probably not doing too well.)

Maybe You Should Avoid the Rising Water (Not Me, You)

I will help you in your weakness. --God

One night in the early 1980s, the lightbulb suddenly came on inside my head again. If we launched the boat on our side of the river, we could cross and take the dog after the many raccoons that were not very accessible from the north side of the river. We were thinking we might get five or six raccoons in one trip. We knew there had been some heavy rains to our west, but again, we did not pay attention to the little things. While we were launching, we wondered where the island was just beyond the ramp. The river was above flood stage. We could see whirlpools in the water just out from the ramp. Kind of scary looking, one of us thought. (Did I mention it was at night?) But no one said anything about giving up, so off we went. We had a pretty good light, so we could see where we were heading, and it did not look good. We were watching and dodging whirlpools on the surface. Some were as large as the boat and about two feet deep. A hole in the water's surface. We actually went into a couple of small ones and felt as if the boat was going to tip. But we had a plan for an enjoyable evening hunting a few raccoons, so we journeyed onward.

About that time, we ran into a very large one. The boat was spun all the way around as if we were heading back to the ramp. We should have kept going, but we got the boat turned to the original heading and went another forty to fifty feet and hit another. We were over halfway across the river by now and had a couple of hundred yards to go. We decided we should heed this second warning and better try to get back to the truck. By now, we were terrified understanding the seriousness of our situation. I reminded my buddies that we knew Jesus pretty close, and now would be a good time to tell him about our need for assistance. I am reminded of an old gospel song that goes like this, "Now let us have a little talk with Jesus, tell him all about our troubles."

As grown men cried, we struggled to get back to the shore. We hit the bank about one hundred yards from the truck. Same as a bull's-eye, we thought. Back is back!

We crept back along the shore to the ramp and got loaded and out of there as quickly as possible. The pains in my side finally subsided after about an hour. Trust me, if you get frightened enough, you will experience a harsh pain in your sides or somewhere. We took a vote among the three of us. We decided that, yes, this was the stupidest thing we had ever done. Looking back thirty-five years, I think and hope this fact doesn't change.

Romans 8:26 - The Spirit of God comes to us and helps us in our weakness.

This verse, no doubt, includes mental weakness or I would have never made it. Fortunately, as I have gotten advanced in years, I installed a switch in my head to turn off the light that suddenly comes on inside my pea brain. Works most of the time.

Chapter 8

The Dogs of McHenry Creek (and One Pony)

I think dogs are the most amazing creatures; they give unconditional love. They are the role model for being alive. —Gilda Radner

Yes, in the late sixties, our dog caught a fish. As mentioned earlier, as youngsters, we spent a lot of time fishing McHenry Creek. Our dog would follow us as we pedaled the mile to the creek. We never purchased a dog. We didn't rescue a dog from the pound. People from the city would just drive out to the country and drop off unwanted animals. This was how we obtained all our pets. We had some great pets. People should never leave animals this way, but we were very grateful. We loved our dogs. We always gave them creative names. From the early sixties, we had a little pup named Kitty-Kitty. We had a cat, and when we started yelling "Here, kitty kitty kitty!" in order to feed her, the little dog would be the first to come a running.

Stray Boy, Blue Boy, and Hey Boy

Then in the late sixties, something very special happened. A very foolish person abandoned and dropped off absolutely the best dog in the history of the world in front of our house one night. We woke up, and there was this beautiful mixed-breed dog. The only thing for sure was it was part collie due to its color. Looking back, it's amazing how smart this dog was. We named him Stray Boy. He went everywhere with us as we played in the area we lived. He would always go fishing with us. One of those Saturday mornings as we fished McHenry, three of the brothers watched as we heard a splash, and Stray Boy was backing up out of the water with a bass weighing about one half of a pound squirming in his mouth. Just about the time the dog had backed completely out of the water, the fish gave a last effort to escape and apparently finned Stray. He yelped and let go. The fish flounced a couple of times and was back into the creek with the dog diving in to attempt to retrieve his prize. We all were cheering for his accomplishment.

One of the greatest dog feats I ever remember was, again, something that Stray Boy did. We were fixing to move into the new house where McHenry started as a spring on the back of the property. Our dad took Stray to the new house and worked there all day trying to get the dog accustomed to his new living quarters. That afternoon, he left him food and water and drove home. It's about six miles. The next morning when we got up to get ready to move some more of our belongings to the new house, there was Stray. He found his way home during the night! Amazing.

Many's the time I would take the dog with me to the big woods behind our house to go squirrel or rabbit hunting. If I shot a squirrel, Stray would run him down and bring him to me. At least two times, I remember him taking off after we jumped a rabbit and, in a few minutes, return with the rabbit in his mouth. He always knew he was better at hunting than me. I did not argue with him.

Finally, he got so old, we lost him one night. Buried him in the back near our pond. Sad day in the history of McHenry Creek.

Not long after, we had another gift dropped off during the night. Another great animal that had a little collie and maybe German shepherd mixed in. He would never replace Stray, but we loved him a long time. Blue Boy. Another great friend for a bunch of young boys. All he wanted to do was play and chase snakes back into the creek.

And then there was Hey Boy. The last in a long line of Boys. We were getting kind of grown by then, so we didn't have as much fun with him as the other two. Anyway, girls started showing up and occupying our time. Hmmm, I wonder if I should have spent more time with the dog.

Tarzan

After we got moved in near the headwaters of McHenry, our grandfather bought a Shetland pony and gave him to us. His name was Tarzan. He stayed mostly in the back fenced lot, but sometimes, we would let him where we played near the house. There was only one absolute with Tarzan; he did not want anyone riding him. We would try, but he would always get rid of us quickly. His favorite method was to scrape you off against a tree as soon as you mounted. He even figured out the clothesline my mom used. One day, a cousin came over.

We were all in the ten-to-fifteen-year range. Cousin jumped on, and Tarzan immediately ran under the clothesline, ripping the intruder from his back. We tried a few more times but finally gave up attempting to ride him. Of course, Stray didn't help by tormenting the mean pony anytime we were out playing. I'm sure the dog thought he was just protecting us.

We put up a basketball goal in the backyard. We spent hours shooting hoops and wishing we could make it go in more by just having fun. Stray and Tarzan would run and nip at our heels playing right along with us. Sometimes when it was quiet for a while, you could watch out the kitchen window and see Tarzan pushing the ball with his nose across the back lot. He would run full speed for seventy to eighty yards at a time and then back toward the house and never let loose of the ball. Sometimes he would find the basketball or football that was low on air and grab it in his teeth and just run with it, shaking his head as he trotted around. As good as he was, we just assumed if he could really pick it up, he would make more baskets than we could.

And then there was the bag swing tied to the big oak. I'm not making this up. My mother had friends of hers watch out the window, some so she could verify it happened. The pony had watched us riding back and forth on the swing, and he figured that if these goofy kids could do it, it must be easy. And there he would go, both front hooves tight to the top of the bag, running with his back feet back and forth just like us. Too bad we didn't have video possibilities back then.

If there are no dogs in Heaven, then when I die I want to go where they went. —Will Rogers

Chapter 9

"Man Overboard"

Actually, the best gift you could have given her was a lifetime of adventures.

—Anonymous (Some think Lewis Carroll, but I can't find it.)

Earlier, I mentioned that my wife likes to throw a quote at me, something about the adventure continuing. You are surely beginning to understand a little about that. I've had many adventures simply by ending up in the water when I was supposed to be in the boat. Best my memory allows, I can confirm that I've fallen out of a boat or intentionally left said boat eleven times. There were various reasons. Some of them were uneventful. I'll skip those.

1. "Did I Tighten All the Screws?"

Back in the day (the seventies), I was rebuilding the front deck on my boat. This included a new seat. After the deck was finished, I was putting the screws into my pedestal. It was a sixteen-inch square fiberglass box with a swivel. The front of the box was open so you could store some of your fishing stuff inside. It had a flange all the way around and holes in each corner for screws. I only had two screws and was in a hurry since we were going fishing as soon as we finished the seat. I put the two screws into the two front holes. I justified not rushing to the shed for more screws by convincing myself I could install the other two in the dark when we got home that night. We arrived at the launch ramp after about a one-hour drive. I slipped on my coveralls, being it was early March and the temperature in the mid-forties. The water temperature was usually upper forties by this time of the year. I climbed into the boat, and my buddy backed me in. The boat floated off, and he pulled up and was heading about fiifty yards up the hill to the parking area. As he got out of the truck, he was startled by my running toward him and screaming as loud as I could to start the truck back up.

As the boat drifted off the trailer, I had leaned forward to lower the electric motor in order to guide the boat over to the shore. I was about thirty-five to forty feet away by then. As I leaned over, the entire pedestal went with me since it did not have screws in the back. I continued going forward and over the front of the boat, seat and all. It was just about six feet deep, so I was able to push myself up from the bottom of the lake and swim to shore in the seemingly freezing water. As soon as my feet hit the bottom, I was running from the water up the hill. By then, my friend had parked the truck and was exiting. I was screaming at him to start it back up and put the heater on high! I jumped into the truck and shed the soaked coveralls. I did not have any extra clothes, so I was at the mercy of the truck's heater. In the meantime, the boat was drifting around out in front of the ramp. Fortunately, the wind was in our favor, and it finally blew it to the shore. I was for leaving the seat and pedestal and getting the boat back onto the trailer and heading for home and dry clothes. My friend convinced me he could recover the seat. After I warmed a little, we backed the trailer near the water. He stripped down to his underwear and waded in. The water was so deep at that point that it was up to his mouth and nose when he finally found the seat with his feet. He went under and worked it back to the shallow water. I was warm enough by now to switch off with him. I backed the trailer in and pulled the boat back in place while he put his dry clothes back on. He then switched to the driver's seat and headed for home as I continued shaking. Another fishing trip ruined by not doing something right the first time.

I reinstalled the seat the next morning, making sure I did not leave anything out this time. (And I started carrying a bag of extra clothes wherever I went.)

"If you don't have time to do it right, when will you have time to do it over?" (John Wooden). Uh, the next day like I said. Please pay attention, John.

2. We Hate Wasps

I guess I will never know why God invented wasps. I don't like them. Not only that, I can't find any good reason we need them. If you find a wasp nest around your house, you spray something on it to kill all the wasps, right? We hate them. It's a universal hate. It's the one thing I believe that everyone agrees on. And it seems they always surprise you. Sometimes you hurt yourself worse by trying to keep from getting stung. I think their only purpose in life is to sting me whenever they get an opportunity. Unfortunately, I have offered them many opportunities.

One pretty spring morning, a buddy of mine and I were going to go fishing in a small oxbow lake just off the Arkansas River. It was very small, and all we needed was an empty flat-bottom and a sculling paddle. We arrived at the lake and pulled the boat out of the truck and into the water. It was a shallow lake with a lot of bushes growing up out of the water. Bushes would extend out away from the shoreline about twenty feet or so. On the other side, it had cypress trees growing in the water. I would paddle in around all the bushes and trees that provided plenty of cover for the many large bass we caught from this lake. For some odd reason, wasps built their nests in the many bushes that grew in the lake. We had been there many times and knew to be careful and, on the lookout, to see them before they saw us. As we drifted out from the bank, I was trying on my favorite spinner bait. I knew there were bushes behind me in the direction the boat was slowly being pushed by the light wind. Just as the boat bumped the brush, I heard that familiar buzz very loudly behind me. There was no doubt to its origin, and I immediately fell over the opposite side of the boat headfirst. It was only about four feet deep, so I stayed under and pushed off with my feet. I came up about twenty feet away. The water where I went under was covered with giant wasps splashing the surface with their wings, wondering where the fresh meat had disappeared. They didn't completely fail as I had been stung four times on my back before I could wash them off by submerging and swimming away. My buddy was leaning back and quivering as he was terrified because he could not swim and felt his chances were better to fight off the wasps instead of drowning. I eased back to the back of the boat and pulled it and him to safety away from the nasty insects. About this time, my back was beginning to burn from the stings.

A couple of hours later, we were on the other side of the lake among the many giant trees. We had caught several bass, and a few were near five pounds. ("A few" sounded better than the actual two we had caught that big.) I was magically guiding the boat around and through the trees with my paddle when I came to a spot I could barely fit the boat between two of the mighty trees. As I passed them, I was looking to my left, not knowing there was a small limb growing directly away from us on the other side of the tree about face-high from the water. Suddenly, the football-size nest was about a foot from my face. I fell backward to get into the water but was blocked by the tree on the other side. That one to two extra seconds was all they needed. As I bounced off the tree to my right, I was swarmed again before I could get over the side and underwater. I stayed close to the boat this time and pushed the boat back away from the danger zone, thus saving my friend again. I stayed in the water, walking beside the boat until we had cleared the trees. I climbed back in and informed him I was done. He agreed, and I paddled back to the truck, giving a wide path from the original nest of angels from hell that was near where we launched. We got the boat back into the bed of the truck and headed for home—and something to stop the stinging sensation all over my back and shoulders. Did I tell you I hate wasps?

I cannot persuade myself that a beneficent and omnipotent God would have designedly created parasitic wasps with the express intention of their feeding within

the living bodies of caterpillars. --Charles Darwin).
What? I'm not sure what that means, but I think Chuck
hates them also.

3. Losing My Balance

This is the number 1 reason for me being overboard so
many times. When you fish in the small boats we do,
you sit on your right leg and sometimes you get to losing
feeling in your legs and feet. I need to stand up
occasionally to stretch and regain the use of the "lost"
limbs. This can be very scary as my fishing partner
must remain quite still in order for me to maintain my
balance and stretch.

During the second spring break when I was the
principal, we went to an old fishing camp along the
White River. Planning on staying all week again, we
rented a small cabin for our headquarters. We threw all
our gear on the beds, food in the fridge, and headed for
the ramp to launch the boat. I motored around to our
cabin. We gathered our fishing equipment and headed
downstream. This was going to be one of those trips
where we motor to a certain spot, pull the boat up on
the bank and tie it off, grab the paddle and rods, and
walk through the woods to a small oxbow with a few
boats tied up. We chose the best one and shoved off.
Turned out the best one was fourteen feet but only
thirty-two inches wide with very shallow sides. In other
words, it was unstable with both of us in it.

We began catching fish immediately. We had circled the
lake once and were heading around again when I raised

myself up to stretch my leg, the one I had been sitting on as I artfully sculled the boat. I was standing with feet apart when I lost my balance. I'm not sure if my fishing partner had shifted or I was just dizzy. Doesn't matter. I was destined to be in the water very quickly. It's not that big of a deal. You just jump up, and the boat will shoot away from you due to the "action-reaction" of physics. That's when the trouble started. The boat was so lightweight that it shot away too quickly. My right foot and leg made it over the side, but my left foot and leg were still in the boat. My right foot settled on the bottom about five feet deep. Again, my left foot hung on the side of the boat. That's what you call the snatch splits—and I couldn't do the splits. Turned out, I had torn everything in the groin area. Tendons, leaders, muscle—everything that could tear, tore. The pain was apparently more than my limit as I fainted and was now floating face down in the water. My partner recognized my dilemma and quickly turned me over, so I would not drown. He then paddled over near the shore, dragging me alongside. When he had dragged me into the mud, he got out of the boat and pulled me up, away from the muddy bank to the dry area.

I was barely coherent, and we were not sure what to do. We decided we would rest a few minutes, and I would probably get to feeling better. As yet, we did not know the extent of my injuries. I pretended to feel better, so we could get back to fishing. I informed him it was his turn to guide the front of the boat. I just lay in the bottom and moaned. He got tired of it after about an hour and decided to head back. He paddled around to the trail and gathered our stuff. The problem now was that when I stood up, I would black out. He carried our fishing poles and paddle back to our boat and came back to get me. I put my arm around his shoulder, and he finally got me back and into the middle of our boat where I could lay down while he motored us back to camp. He helped me up to the cabin where I could lay down on the bed. He went to the guy's house that ran this camp and came back with some OTC pain meds. The label said to take two, so I took two doses.

He showered and fixed some supper. The NCAA Final basketball game was on TV, so we ate while watching. He finally went to bed and started his usual ritual of snoring and keeping me awake. I could not sleep anyway. I knew I was in trouble but did not want to leave.

About an hour later, I needed to pee really bad. I decided I would work my way to the front porch where I could hang on to a post holding up the roof and lean forward and take care of business. This put me in such a strain that urination was out of the question. I hobbled back to bed. Now I needed to go worse. I crawled back to the front porch and tried again. Nothing! I concluded that I was in pretty bad shape. I knew I needed medical attention but was not sure what steps to take to accomplish that.

After exhausting every scenario, I decided the only way I could relieve myself was to roll over against the wall and pee off the side of the bed into the wall. It worked. I felt sure that it would soak through the cracks in the floor before anyone noticed.

As it finally became light outside, I yelled at fishing buddy to wake up and take me home, so I could get some help. He pulled the truck around to the ramp and walked back to the cabin to get into the boat and motor around to load up. The boat was gone. The river had risen about a foot during the night, and we forgot to tie the boat with all the confusion of my being hurt. He ran down to the launch area, and a couple of guys were putting their boat in and agreed to take him downstream to retrieve our boat. They found it about a mile downstream, just drifting along.

We got loaded up and headed for the nearest drugstore in a small town in the area. The pharmacist gave me some ibuprofen and told me to take four. I did, and we headed for home. Sometimes when it comes to fishing, we don't make the best decisions. I got to feeling better about halfway home, and we pulled into another lake to try fishing for a while. That lasted about two hours, and my pain meds wore off. I informed him that I really was done this time and to take me home no matter what I said otherwise. We got home about dark.

I took a bunch of meds, took a bath, and went to bed. Next morning, I pretended I was doing better so my wife would go to work. I then got in my truck and drove to my mother's house and had her take me to my doctor. I forced my way in, having no appointment. My doctor at the time was kind of a quack and a clown. He talked to me a few minutes while looking me over and informed me that this would be the first dislocated crotch he had ever dealt with. He asked me why I waited this long before getting help. I informed him that I did not understand the question. He gave me some special pain medicine and sent me to a physical therapist to deal with me.

As I awoke the next morning, I was sure something was wrong due the abnormal dizziness I was displaying. My wife noticed my back was black and blue. I soon discovered the discoloration was from the center of my back down to my left heel. Back to the doctor. They ran some tests and found that I was between two to three units of blood low due to the internal bleeding. More meds and back to bed.

By the next Monday, I was able to get to school but was confined to a wheelchair for a week, then crutches for two weeks, and a cane for a few days after that.

(Still looking for the "fishing is fun" guy.)

"Is there anyone so wise as to learn by the experience of others?" (Voltaire).

I hope you're paying attention.

4. Losing My Balance Again

I've been asked many times as to the success of my fishing. Let me spell it out to you in just a few steps.

Step 1. Confirm with my nephew that we are going in the morning.

Step 2. Pick him up and head east to lower White River.

Step 3. Arrive and launch boat.

Step 4. Motor to slough that leads to lake.

Step 5. Remove 9.9 Evinrude and tank and hide in bushes.

Step 6. Drag boat over beaver dam.

Step 7. Start catching fish.

So far, everything was going well. We were catching fish and having a great time. As usual, I was giving him a harsh fishing lesson. He was fishing, and I was catching. We had been at it for a few hours when I stood up just to stretch and get the blood flowing in my legs. I still can't confirm that it was intentional, but he shifted around in the back seat, and I was about to go over the side again. Both of my rods were on the side that I was fixing to exit the boat, so I attempted a world-class dive into the water in an effort to not break my fishing tools. It worked in that my rods were not broken, but I ended up going in headfirst in water that was two and a half feet deep.

These old lakes are a hundred years old and have become silted by leaves and small limbs during their lifetime. If you were to crawl out of your boat and attempt to walk, you would be near knee-deep in an instant. The bottom is very soft.

Now, I am on my hands and knees with my head sticking straight down into the mud and silt. I try to push down with my hands, but they sink to my elbows. This is getting a little scary, realizing there is no air below the bottom of the lake. I feel I have one chance. I pull my knees up to my chest with my toes pointing straight back with legs together. This gives me more flat surface to push against the mud. I simultaneously push up with my legs and palms. I can feel my head inching upwards. Being stuck has caused a suction between my head and the mud. Fortunately, my head continues to slowly rise from the watery muddy grave. I thrust my head upwards and take a deep breath. I look around at the back of the boat and asked my former favorite nephew what he was waiting for? He informs me that he had wondered what was taking so long for me to get back in the boat. He told me I was holding him up. He had fished out the area and was ready to move down the shoreline a little farther. He figured I had spooked all the fish in this area anyway by splashing around. I asked him if he had not realized that I was stuck in the bottom of the lake and needed help. He said no, and while I was still sitting in the mud, I might consider washing all the mud from my face and head. I told him I could not move as I had lost my glasses from being stuck in the mud, and if I moved, I would lose my bearing of where I had lost them. I splashed water in my face to remove as much mud as possible and started reaching my hands into the silty mud until I actually found my glasses. I was careful in working them back up from under about a foot of the mud. I finally washed off pretty well and worked my way back into the boat. We continued catching more fish for several more hours.

Step 8. Head back to the beaver dam and pull boat back over.

Step 9. Reinstall motor and gas tank.

Step 10. Motor back to launch ramp.

Step 11. Wade into water deep enough to completely wash all the dried mud from my entire body and clothes.

Step 12. Change into fresh clothes I now carry with me everywhere I go.

Step 13. Load boat and head home.

Fishing is easy, just follow the steps.

Remember what Bilbo used to say. *It's a dangerous business, Frodo, going out your door. You step onto the road, and if you don't keep your feet, there's no knowing where you might be swept off to.* --J. R. R. Tolkien

5. Two at a Time

I enjoy going overboard so much I have invited others. A friend and I were at it again one night at a small but very clear lake. We had caught very few bass, so I decided to shine my spotlight into the water to see if I could find some fish that way. We actually were now seeing a few, and that pesky light in my head came on again. I knew I had a frog gig in my truck. I had a ladder rack, and the gig was tied on top. You never know when a good gig will come in handy. We agreed that this was one of those times. We cranked up the motor and took off to the truck.

It did not take long before we were attempting to gig a few fish. Small fish were everywhere, and it appeared the larger fish that we had a chance to spear were going to be gar. Game fish like bass and crappie are too smart to hang around after a bright beam of light hits them. (Actually, right now I'm just trying to throw off any game wardens that might be reading. Not sure if the statute of limitations for gigging fish at night has run out since the mid-1970s.)

We did gig a few gar. And suddenly, we were faced with the largest bluegill (bream) we had ever seen. Now it is possible that the clear water that was about ten feet deep was magnifying the size, but it was still big. We decided it would be a shame to not attempt to capture this record-size fish. We leaned forward, me reaching with the gig and my friend pointing the light. The gig was only twelve feet long, so I had to lean pretty far. We were drifting ever closer, and suddenly, I thrust the gig with all my might. The problem now was that we were leaning so far that when I lunged forward, the boat shot straight back, and we were now doing a swan dive off the front deck of the boat. Come to find out, there is something to that action-reaction math equation.

We bobbed to the top, and my partner was swimming toward the bank about twenty feet away. I followed just to crawl up on the bank and catch my breath. After a few minutes of debating whose fault it was, I waded back in and swam for the boat that was now about fifty yards away.

After getting the boat back to the bank and picking him up, we positioned the boat over the spot of the crime. The light was still shining, but it was about ten feet down on the bottom. I stared at him for a minute but agreed it could have possibly been more my fault than his. So, I dove back in and retrieved the light and gig. We decided that the fun had worn off this trip, so we headed for the ramp and loaded up and went home.

But I did have dry clothes to change into. At least I learned one lesson during the seventies.

Curiouser and curiouser! —Lewis Carroll, Alice in Wonderland

Chapter 10

Snakes and Other Creepy Things

There was a story from Aesop Fables about a man who found a snake up on a cold mountain. The snake, being cold-blooded, was about to die. The man felt sorry for him and picked it up to carry it to a warm place down below. When the snake warmed up, he gave the man a vicious deadly bite. As the man lay dying, he asked the snake why he bit him after he had helped the snake. The snake replied, "It's your fault. You knew I was a snake when you picked me up."

Stay away from snakes. --God (Well, I'm sure he said something like that.)

Over thousands of years, many people confuse Satan with a snake. Not sure that's real. The Bible does refer to Satan when mentioning a serpent. Not sure that is the same thing we should think of when we talk about snakes. There are definitely some bad snakes out there. Some of them are reptiles.

Cuz versus the Serpent (Bitten by a Rattlesnake)

Being bitten by a snake runs in the family. We don't play with them or anything like that; it's just happened a couple of times. Sometime about 1966, my cousin and I were eleven and twelve years old. We had walked from his house and were fishing a small pond in what was at the time the newest area known as West Little Rock. It was just off Markham and a little east of Shackelford.

Old-timers will recognize the spot, just across Markham from The Tiawana Supper Club. You know, right where Highway 430 crosses under. We were wearing our normal fishing attire: cutoff jeans and tennis shoes. I'm sure we actually owned shirts back then, but we seemed to never wear them. We were having a good time walking the bank and catching a few small bass when this lady came out of the house nearby and shouted at us that we weren't supposed to be there. I'm certain her next comment was going to be something about if we needed anything to drink, but we had taken off by then, running as fast as we could to get away from the wicked witch of the west. Our story would not be entertaining to our friends if we had to say she was nice or fluff like that.

It was going to be a short run. All we had to do was leave the southwest area of the pond we were fishing and head back north to the street. It was definitely a wooded area but still not very far, maybe one hundred yards or less. The problem was that there was a lot of weeds and light brush growing all over the ground. And full of spiderwebs. We were the same height, so we were both getting a face full of nasty webs. I think I paused first and asked him to lead the way. I was hoping he would fall for this and therefore tear down the webs, so I would have a clear path for my face. It worked. He started off. We were now about twelve to fifteen yards from stepping out into someone's backyard. Cuz yelled, jumped about seven feet high, and took off running as fast as he could to the house in front of us. The last thing I heard him say was "Snake!" All that I was sure of now was that there was some giant biblical monster between me and safety. I started beating the ground in front of me with my fishing rod. I was now sweating profusely. I felt certain I was going to wet my pants soon. Suddenly, I caught a glimpse of something moving to my left. There he went, a seventeen-foot long creepy crawler that I was sure had been cursed by God. I immediately started running and leaping just in case there was a pair of them. When I got into the clear, I heard my cousin crying and shouting to the elderly lady that had opened the back door. He was informing her that a monster has bitten him, and it was not even Halloween. The old husband had now showed up, and I could hear him saying something about putting a tourniquet on it. I wasn't sure what that meant, but I remember hoping that it didn't burn as much as putting alcohol on a cut.

Cuz finally remembered his phone number, and the lady called his mother to come get us. Medical advances weren't as good back then, and I think he spent a week in the hospital. They were having trouble deciding what kind of snake had bitten him. Surprisingly, they could not find one in their science books that grew to seventeen feet in our area. I told them repeatedly that I got a good look at it, and yes, it was at least that long. They assured me they believed me but were perplexed at my inability to remember its color after having such a good look at it. After some testing, it was determined it was indeed a rattlesnake that had poisoned him to near death.

There was a time in the first few days that his ankle had swollen so large that they were going to start lancing the ankle and foot if the swelling did not go down. I guess it was going to explode or something due to growing so large. I remember thinking, Gross, I sure am glad he took the lead and knocked down all those spiderwebs.

"I'd rather be lucky than good." --Lefty Gomez

I'm Still Alive! (Bitten by a Cottonmouth)

"Be alert, be on watch! Your enemy, the Devil, roams around like a roaring lion, looking for someone to devour."
--Good News Bible

The devil tried to kill me again. And this time, he came in person! I was bitten by a giant snake on July 31, 2015. I was wade-fishing a creek that feeds into the Buffalo River with my brother. Probably not a good idea with my knee in the shape it's in, but it sounded good at the time. We met under a bridge and left from there. We had been fishing about three hours and were about a mile or two from the trucks when we decided it was about time to turn back. I told him, "Let's try the next tailwater," being it was a little darker—which meant deeper. It could hold the biggest fish of the day. We walked around the rapids and a few weeds and were getting close when I noticed he was cutting me off. Just like kids again, always competitive in trying to get in the first cast. He stepped in and made his cast. I was right behind him, and I stepped into the stream from the gravel bank area. I stepped on a slippery rock, I guess, and both feet shot forward out from under me. I landed about the center of my back on the shoreline. I threw both arms out to brace my fall, and my right arm landed right on top of a coiled cottonmouth. He was fishing also, and I disturbed him. He was coiled right beside the bank, ready to strike a perch for lunch. Twenty minutes earlier, we had seen a big cottonmouth swimming up the creek with a perch in its mouth.

I was sitting in the water when he struck me just below the right elbow. I rolled to my left to get away from him. Being crippled with arthritis, I wasn't able to jump up. I hollered at my brother for help, and he replied, "Hang on, I've got one." After reeling in his fish, he reached to grab my left arm to help me up, and I told him I had been bitten. He kind of laughed at me, so I turned my elbow toward him. (I had not looked yet.) In all seriousness as only he can do, he said, "Well, that's either a snake or a vampire." I rolled my arm, so I could see. Blood was flowing down my arm from both fang marks. I was immediately devastated. We were wading and left our phones in the truck. No picture of the bleeding fangs!

We tied a bandanna around my arm just above the elbow. He walked just ahead and to my right in order to elevate the arm. After a few steps, he asked if it was true that medical people had stopped recommending to cut the point of bite and suck out the poison. I assured him that was true, and he said, "Good."

We walked the sixty minutes to the trucks and headed for the medical facility in a nearby town. We found it closed. Only open Monday to Thursday. He told me there was another medical facility in the town, so we headed that direction. I pulled up and saw cars. I was starting to feel better. I parked and walked to the receptionist desk and informed her I had been attacked by a deadly serpent. She acted startled but told me they could not help due to the fact that they were the County Health Department. I asked her what people in this area would do if they were bitten by snakes on the weekend, just die? She said they would drive forty miles to the nearest hospital. I sent my brother home since he lived north, and I was heading south. I started the forty-mile trip to the ER. (I kept my streak alive as well. This was my eighteenth ER visit, and I had driven myself every time except when I was too young to drive, and my mother took me.)

I contacted another brother near home to let him know what was going on. Made sure he knew that if I called back and was not coherent, he might have to call 911 and inform them of my plight. My arm was rapidly swelling and was beginning to hurt. I arrived at the ER about 5:00 p.m. I parked up front where doctors park and rushed inside. The lady informed me I must drive around back to the ER. I told her I was too dizzy, and she must take me through the hospital to ER. We made two turns, and she pointed at a door for me to enter. It was the financial office. I had to fill out paperwork! Looking back, I should have fallen to the floor and started quivering. Once in the ER, they drilled me with a tetanus shot first thing. After nine attempts, they finally got an IV installed. (I knew they were having trouble with it, but the paramedic on the ambulance I rode to Little Rock later saw it in my folder and commented they must have had trouble.) They were administering an antivenom through the IV. After they got it hooked up, they put me in an ambulance and transferred me to

Baptist ER in Little Rock. I spent forty-eight hours there. Come to find out, cottonmouth venom ain't good for you. I threw up for two days. The attending doctor at the hospital told me I could go home when I could keep some food down. I tried a few Cheerios and water Saturday morning. Didn't last ten seconds. At lunch, I took one bite of a sandwich. Again, ten seconds. By supper, I got the shakes just by looking at food.

It was not a pretty experience. I was holding a vomit bucket in one hand and a plastic container to pee in with the other. I was not able to stand and walk to the bathroom. Horrible seasickness. After puking for over twenty-four hours, they brought me a breakfast burrito Sunday morning. I swooned and asked for more Cheerios. Well, that didn't work either. I was on the verge of believing that "upchucking" was my new hobby. Finally, about 1:00 p.m., after eating a couple of bites of a sandwich, I realized after about ten minutes, I was keeping it down. I ate half of the lunch in order to please the doctor and was able to head home about 4:30 p.m., arm still swollen beyond recognition.

I received a call from the doctor's office Monday afternoon. They informed me that after analyzing my latest bloodwork, I was not going to lose my right arm. Good, first I heard of that possibility. They informed me they didn't want to upset me with all the specifics until they were sure.

The fact of the matter is that Jesus bailed me out again. I'm always looking for pennies lying around on the ground and in parking lots. It works. You should try it.

(Read the poem "Pennies from Heaven" by C. Mashburn sometime.)

And one more thing for Satan. Snakebite? Really? You gotta do better than that!

On the bright side, Terry has never been stung by a scorpion, received a bite from a spider, attacked by a piranha, mauled by a bear, pounced upon by a mountain lion, or eaten by a dinosaur. (But then again, he's only sixty-two.)

Chapter 11

About Swimming Pools

The Versatile Boat (Imagination)

*Think left and think right and think low and think high.
Oh, the things you can think up if only you try!* —Dr.
Seuss

A lot of people have swimming pools. I've never had the kind of pool you are thinking of, but we did have a rural Arkansas pool when we were small children. My mother still has a picture. It was the talk of the neighborhood. (As in they made fun of us because of our pool.) By some standards, we would have been labeled as poor people. We didn't know we were poor. We weren't hungry or dirty, but there were not some of the "extras" that most folks enjoy these days. I think at Christmas, we just assumed Santa Clause was just always mad at us or something. Anyway, we had heard that he didn't leave much for mean kids. So, we got over it. No matter our worldly status, we were happy. We had fun no matter what else. We could always find a way to enjoy our circumstances. It's called imagination.

It gets hot in the summer in central Arkansas. Humidity adds to the swelter. So hot and sweaty was the norm for kids growing up when we did. There was no staying inside to watch TV or play video games. We had neither. I think our first little black-and-white thirteen-inch TV came when I was about nine or ten years old. We didn't have an air-conditioner till much later, so staying inside was no bargain. So, we did like everyone else did in the summer; we had peanut butter–covered pancakes with homemade syrup for breakfast, and our mom ran us outside till time for a sandwich at lunch.

We had a small aluminum boat out by the back fence. (Of course we did.) One afternoon during late June, our dad dragged it up close to the house and stuck the water hose over in it and turned it on. Probably took about twenty minutes to fill it up. Instant swimming pool. Swimming pools don't have to be round in order to have fun in the water. We were sure that folks named Rockefeller wished they had it made like us.

The Versatile Truck (Maximum Teenager)

I've heard big-mouthed blowhard guys tell the story of filling the bed of their truck with water and call it a swimming pool. I'm sure most are lying. But there are pictures on the Internet now, so someone has. Well, let's get something straightened out once and for all. I invented that in July 1975. The Internet doesn't go back that far, so those pictures were not of me. I did not invent the Internet, but one Saturday night in July at the Kroger parking lot on University Avenue, right across from UALR, I pulled my truck out of the alley behind the Town and Country strip mall with a bed full of water and a girlfriend splashing around in the back.

Keep in mind, I had a big truck for the times. A 1970 Chevy three-quarter ton with a positive trac rear end. It had a four speed with a granny low. It was a real work truck. It had sixteen-and-a-half-inch wheels when nothing else did. There was a full-service gas station just west of an apartment complex, which was just west of Town and Country. I had already cut some large pieces of plastic sheeting that I could lay in the bed just right, so it would cover the entire bed and up the walls of the bed just to the top. I pulled into the gas station and rolled out my plastic liner and ran about eight inches of water into the bed. That was plenty as I figured it would be filled with pretty girls in a few minutes, which would raise the water level. My girlfriend was only five feet three inches and weighed about ninety pounds, so she did not overflow the sixty-five-degree water in my pool. As I pulled out onto the street, I could tell I was loaded down due to the weight of the water. I turned in behind the little mall and eased up the alley. When we came into view of the parking lot, I started hearing shouts, screams, and cheers from the many teenagers and folks in their early twenties. We didn't have much to do back then, so hanging out in parking lots was normal.

This particular parking lot was famous for holding truck pulls. Guys who were influenced by their peers, and the presence of the many pretty girls, would back their trucks up toward each other and hook a chain on both trailer hitches. They would proceed to ease away from each other until the chain was tight. That's when the hollering and sound of tires squealing began. That's when these two guys would pop their clutches and see who had the best truck. (Whatever that meant.)

I pulled my truck into one of the crowded parking spots and shut it off. Guys and gals began to make their way over to see. Everyone kind of figured out what was going on, so girls started climbing up the bumper and over the tailgate and into the water. Eleven. That's how many girls wearing cutoffs and T-shirts were now sitting in the cold water filling my wonderful swimming pool. My truck bed was now surrounded three rows deep of fellows with bug eyes. This is a family book, so you will have to use your imagination at this time. One of my friends eased over to me, elbowed me in the side, and said, "You're my hero." Yes, I was.

If you never did, you should. These things are fun, and fun is good. —Maximum Teenager

(Actually, I read it in a Dr. Seuss book.)

The End

Wherever you go, no matter what the weather, always bring your own sunshine.

—Anthony J. D'Angelo

The McHenry Creek Fishers Users Guide and Dictionary

If you ain't from where we grew up, pay attention, it may take you a while to catch on.

%#*#$! - A term used when the biggest bass of your life gets away. Same term may be used when a small one gets away. Also interchangeable with the term for getting a hook stuck into your finger. Usually involves mumbling.

A.A. Milne & Dr. Seuss - Terry's favorite authors.

Backlash - Your spool blows up and ruins your line. Also known as a wasp's nest to bass fisherman. It happens when you don't have your drag set right. Or if you attempt to cast too hard into the wind. Or, if you simply do not know what you are doing. Usually followed by saying "%#*#$!"

Balloons - *No one can be uncheered with a balloon. --* Winnie the Pooh
I hear people every day talking about having a bad day. Most of the time, their bad day is merely a simple temporary inconvenience. Truly having a "bad day" would be the loss of a loved one, divorce, tornado damage, truck stolen, or worse your boat... that sort of stuff. Those "temporary" inconveniences can be overcome by something as simple as getting yourself a balloon and writing some good thoughts on it with a marker and hanging it in a prominent place at home. If

you think you are having a bad day, read a Dr. Seuss book or Google some Winnie the Pooh quotes. Works every time.

Also, Terry likes to have a little orange color on his spinner baits. The bass that choose to habitat the many oxbows in southeast Arkansas love crawdads. These mudbugs have a little orange tint to them. If Terry is out of bright orange fingernail polish to paint the heads of his spinner baits, he cuts up orange balloons and places strips on his hook for his trailer. This kind of outlandish behavior causes Terry's friends and brothers to say "%#*#$!" They can criticize all they want, it works. Terry has pictures.

Bike Racing - The act of riding your bike as fast as you can in order to get to the creek first and therefore have a chance to catch the first fish of the day.

Blowed up on - Also known as the Commode Flusher! The act of running your buzz bait, frog, Lucky 13, or other top water bait across the top of some Lilly pads or a weed bed and a good-sized bass blows up the surface of the water attempting to get your bait.

Bobber - Normally thought of as a device placed a couple of feet above your hook that is baited with a minnow or even worse, a bug. (See PJ) After living most of my life in person, I understand the term to mean something quite differently. The "Bobber" is the guy that goes underwater to retrieve a motor after it has been lost from back of boat. When he "Bobs" up with the motor, it's a good day! (Makes sense if you read my fishing adventure book!)

Another meaning is also recognized. After falling from the boat again, the act of "bobbing" up to catch your breath in order to climb back into the boat or swim to shore. (Yeah, you'll find out all about that in the same book.)

Actually, there is one more use of the idea of bobber or bobbing up. Terry has very poor eyesight. His best eye is twenty over five hundred. That means he cannot see the giant E at the top of the eye chart. Early one morning as he and one of his friends were easing the boat through some brush to get to one of their favorite lakes. A small limb kicked back and knocked his glasses from his face. The water was nearly six feet deep. Terry's friend peeled off his clothes and slipped over the side of the boat to retrieve them. The water was a little dingy and he would not be able to see the bottom, so diving under was out of the question. He simply tip toed around the area until one his toes touched the glasses. He grasped them with his toes and attempted to bend his knee in order to reach the glasses with his hand. As soon as he raised his feet from the bottom, he went under. He suddenly BOBBED up with the glasses in hand! Terry was relieved. Not just because he got his glasses back but that his friend actually came back up and did not succumb to any bad things happening to him. You know, if he was not able to return to the surface and continue living, the fishing trip would have been over.

Boat Cracking - Most folks have heard of "Safe Cracking." It's a reference to a bad guy attempting to rob someone's safe. Well, we don't usually try to break into anyone's safe, although we have "borrowed" a few boats and an occasional truck. Boat Cracking is not really an art or special gift, it just takes a little experience and to be a little mechanically inclined. My family and friends have spent a lot of fishing trips on the lower White River Basin fishing in small sloughs, canals, oxbow lakes and the like. Many of these trips involve motoring on the river itself or launching on some of the old river channels called "bays." Sometimes you have to motor a few miles to get to your destination. We would look on maps and navigational charts (this was 20-30 years ago so Google Earth was not an option) for the many oxbows and fishing holes a little ways off the river. Sometimes we would drag our boat over to the small lake. This would only be done if the lake was very close. I built an axle mounted on two motorcycle wheels, so we could roll our boat to these lakes. You simply pull up onto the shore, hide your motor and gas tank, pull your boat up onto the axle and start rolling it like a two-wheel cart.

What we hoped for was that there would be a few boats (or at least one) tied up at the lake that we were planning on fishing. You would just untie the boat and push off having brought a paddle with you and start fishing. The problem with that was that the boat owners started using chains and locks to secure their boats. Now extreme measures come into play. You would have to plan and be prepared for this type rudeness. So I carried a backpack along, my "boat cracking" kit.

The contents of the backpack are thus:

<u>KIT "A"</u> - Bolt cutters and several locks. I would find a boat that was chained to a tree and cut a link from the chain and add my lock. Now when I returned to this lake I could unlock my lock and fish. It was common practice, there were usually 5 or 6 locks already attached to the chain owned by other clever fisherman.

<u>KIT "B"</u> - Several sizes of nuts and bolts and 2 crescent wrenches, one for standard size and one for metric. The chain used to secure the boat had to run through one of the handles on the front or back of the boat. Many times these were bolted on. You simply remove the nut with your wrench and go fishing. If the handle was attached to the boat by rivets, you had to find a way to break the metal rivet off the boat. I found that the easiest way was to pick up the opposite end of the boat from the tree it was chained to, back up so the chain was slightly extended, and the boat was a couple of feet off the ground, ease forward and then step back and yank the boat as hard as you can. The weight of the boat would then snap off the rivet holding the chain. Now you can go fishing. When I had properly fished out the small lake, we would drag the boat back to the tree and install our own nuts and bolts into the hole in the handle where the rivet broke out and re-secure the chain. No one would notice the difference between a rivet and a bolt.

Borry something - To take and use something that

belongs to someone else for a period of time before returning it. Well, that doesn't sound so bad. We've borried a boat or three under that definition. Hey, even a truck or two. We always put them back. They were even still useable when we finished with them. One day we needed to pull my truck up out of the river after I had backed in a little too far attempting to put the boat back on my trailer. Some guy had left the keys in his truck, so we figured he wouldn't mind. I even thought he was probably just a real good Christian man and left it there for others to use if they needed to.

Bucket Mouth - This is an old description of big bass. Their proper name is Largemouth bass, so Bucket Mouth. (Well, that's a pretty good description of the ones Terry catches.)

Although, there is another description. If you attempt to go fishing too much, you might have to listen to some legitimate concerns from your wife.

Bugs - There are many bugs known by many names. Pests is one. I believe this term is short for pestilence, a word used in the Bible with various meanings. It was one of the plagues used against Egypt.

There are a few different references to bugs for fishermen and women. One is the mosquito. Nasty little flying bugs that bite. They go after you every time you go fishing in warmer weather.

And there's the chigger. They are bothersome when fishing from creek banks. They usually bite you around the ankles and make you scratch and cause your skin to become raw. The quick recovery is alcohol. (Not the drinking kind) Just rub it on the bites. It soothes the burning and itching. The more permanent solution to chigger bites is putting some bleach in your bathwater and soak those ankles for a while.

Then there is the worst bug of all, the biting fly! They seem to always be around small flat bottom boats. When we walk over to an oxbow, borry the boat that has been left there, and start fishing, those flies from hell begin their mission of making your life as miserable as possible. You are barely able to fish for fighting them off. You will have many welts after fishing for several hours, all of them bleeding. May cause you to say %#*#$!

Then there's the fishing bugs. Most PJs use crickets to bream fish. In the old days we dug up another kind of bug, worms. As you become a more accomplished fisherman, you hang up the lesser fishing equipment and go after big bass. Fishing with bugs is more of a kids and beginners way of catching small fish.

Therefore, if someone refers to you as a PJ, it is probably not meant to be a compliment.

Daycare - A place where parents leave their children in order to go to work or shopping. This is usually a place where someone charges you a set rate per day. This term was not known or used in the mid to late 1960s. Daycare back then was our mom fixing some pancakes covered in peanut butter and homemade syrup. After we finished eating she would shoo us out of the house. We would then jump on our bikes and head to McHenry Creek as fast as possible. When we got hungry, we would head back for a sandwich and then play ball in the corner lot up the road or go back to the creek for the rest of the afternoon. Sooner or later we would drag back to the house to clean up and eat supper. Then just hit replay the next morning.

Dog fish - A species of medium size shark. Having never lived around the ocean, we didn't know that in 1967. We just knew that our dog could catch a fish. After spending many days following us up and down McHenry Creek observing, he dove into the water one morning and came out with about a half pound bass in his mouth. I bet you a roll of duct tape that your dog never accomplished such a feat.

Duct Tape - Something that can be used to barter with. One of the essential elements needed in order to get through life. If you had to choose on which to carry with you to sustain life, a roll of duct tape or a bottle of Vitamin C, no contest. It's hard to get through a day without needing some duct tape for something. You may have to tape a broken rod back together in order to continue fishing. The little latch on the box I carried my extra fishing lures was broken. I used duct tape to keep it closed. My set of the Lord of the Rings Trilogy I purchased in 1969 for instance, the paperback covers are torn off the books. I used duct tape to secure them back to the books. What are you going to use to tape up the splices after rewiring your trolling motor connections to the battery in the back of the boat? You don't really think I would drive to a hardware store for a roll of electrical tape?

Everyone knows that band aids won't hold on the finger you just stuck a hook into unless you use duct tape to secure it. How else would you fix your vacuum cleaner hose without it? By the way, what else would you use to hold the batteries in your tv remote? Patch a hole in your tent? Hold up posters on your bedroom wall?

Terry even used duct tape to wrap tightly around his right forearm that was broken after he fell in 2016 attempting to get into his boat. It only worked about an hour before the pain sent him running for home. But, he got to fish for an hour. Glorious duct tape saved part of the day.

He even used an entire roll to hold my broken boat trailer axle to the frame, so I could drive home one night. And what else could you use to replace the glass for your truck door after it has been broken out, huh?

Even Matt Damon referenced it on the movie *The Martian: Duct tape is magic and should be worshiped.* Not sure if I would go that far, but I know what he means.

Fisherman - See Liar.

Fishing buddy - These are the guys that line up to have an opportunity to go fishing with Terry. He has spent a lifetime as one of the most prolific bass fishermen of all time. There are so many lesser guys who enjoy fishing and want to go with him, that Terry can't remember all their names. So, the term fishing buddy is simply used for convenience.

If you go to Terry's website, you can send him a request to go on a fishing adventure with him. Really. MchenryCreekFishers.com

Griz - A scary fish commonly known as a Grinnell throughout the South and it is technically known as a Bowfin. A ferocious predator with a mouth full of razor sharp teeth which usually destroys perfectly good spinnerbaits. Its name may come from the movie Jeremiah Johnson. During the movie Jeremiah was asked if he could skin Griz. (Referring to a grizzly bear) When a Grinnell blows up on your bait and you miss him your buddy will ask; what's the matter, you can't catch Griz?

Grinnell Knocker - My personal knocker was a one and one quarter inch wooden rod about three feet long. We very seldom carried a net and when you get a five or six-pound Griz to the boat, it is imperative that you are able to defend yourself.

Also substitutes for a Yo Yo knocker. It is illegal to leave yo yos unattended and as we found such, we simply took it upon ourselves to teach the perpetrator a lesson. Game wardens can't be everywhere, and we were happy to help out.

By the way. Who told you that hanging yo yos was fishing? If you ain't got a rod and reel in your hand, YOU AIN'T FISHIN'! (That means I was screaming at you!) Yes, Yo Yos make me want to say "%#*#$!"

Having a good day: This one is simple, going fishing! Most men believe that having a good day has something to do with keeping their wives happy. Terry also believes that is a key ingredient to happiness. If Carla's happy, Terry may get to go fishing.

Hooked - As in; "I'm hooked on fishing." Or, "%#*#$! I've hooked myself again!"

Landing - Most of the time this is a reference to getting your fish to the boat. It also can indicate where you launched your boat. Or, it can be used after you were running to get to your boat after launching and tying it up to the dock. You slip on a slick board that connects the bank to the dock and after a couple of flips and a twist; you "stick the landing" on the edge of the dock. This is followed by crying and holding on to the affected area of your body where the bones may be broken. This will NOT be followed by saying %#*#$! as you will be unable to speak for several minutes.

Liar - Refers to most fishermen. (At least ninety percent) It's amazing. These guys simply can't tell the truth. They always exaggerate their catch. If you don't see pictures, they are lying. Don't believe anything they tell you. Well Terry doesn't lie about his catch, he's very good at fishing and his stories can always be taken seriously.

As an example, JB and I were heading to a medium sized lake to catch some bass. On the gravel road leading to the launching ramp we met a lake ranger. I had met him many times, so we stopped to talk for a minute. We mentioned we had caught some white bass in this lake. He informed us that they had been active in the lake for a while. He also told us that he has caught two over 7 pounds! My brother asked to see the pictures. He replied that it wasn't a big deal and he didn't have any pictures. He has told his lie so much, he now believes it to be true. We said "goodbye" and headed for the ramp.

The problem with his statement is this: a 7-pound white bass would be the world's record!!!! And he's caught two?

We assume he has to carry extra clothes wherever he goes.

"Liar, Liar, Pants on fire!"

Ole Grinder - The name for my Zebco 33 I began my fishing career with. No matter how much Vaseline you put on those gears, you could not get them to quit making that grinding noise as you retrieved your lure or in my case your fish. I attest that it was simply worn out due to catching so many fish.

One Cranker - If you have a good outboard motor you know what this means. If you have to crank and pull the starting rope quite a few times, you need a better motor. If you do not understand this concept, it simply means that you are young and didn't realize that motors didn't used to have electric starters.

Pestilence - This term is interchangeable with high wind and many other natural disasters that mess up a good fishing day. Believe me, the earth is cursed...says so in the Bible. I can believe it from all the bad things that can happen to you because you love to fish. How many times have you left home pulling your boat and trailer, and the wind seems calm? Upon arriving at the lake, you wonder how you missed the gale force wind warnings on the weather channel.

Sometimes, it seems that no matter which direction you are attempting to fish, the wind is in your face again. But heed this: no matter how much fishermen complain about the wind, I'd rather fight the wind than calm water. Bass feed better with some kind of ripple on the water. The calm water seems to make them skittish. However, sometimes that ripple is known as white capping swales and you better be careful. But if you can tough it out, there are bass to be caught in the rough water.

PJ - Perch Jerker. Someone who attempts to catch small *pan fish*. This person will resort to any tactic they can to catch a fish, using all manner of bugs and minnows with, cover your ears, bobbers! This is also an angler who is not as prolific as Terry is at catching big bass, so they have to do what they have to do in order to catch enough fish for supper. (He said bobbers)(But he didn't say %#*#$!)

Plug - A fishing lure. The artificial bait you are casting. There are many varieties so pick out your favorite and start chunkin'.

Also known as what keeps the water out of your boat. You fishermen think I was talking about the store-bought plug that fits perfectly in the hole in the back of the boat in order to drain it after a rain or if your boat leaks. Well, I wasn't, everyone knows about that. I'm talking about the stick you put in the hole in the bottom of the boat you just shoved off the bank of an oxbow lake you walked 20 minutes to get to. Sometimes mean people would punch holes in boats left on these lakes. A little hole in the bottom never stopped us. You simply find a stick or a root that sort of fits in the hole and push the boat in the water. Although the fishing buddy in the back may have to hold his foot on it to keep it from coming out and sinking the boat.

If you know you have a hole like that in your boat you can fix it ahead of time. Simply put silicone around the stick and let it cure overnight. Works like new!

Rudder - A device that allows your boat to be steered or guided along the bank line as you fish. If you do not have a rudder, and you are sculling your small boat, the back end will try to come around and pass the front end. If you have an outboard motor on the back, that's all you need. However, if you walk over to the many oxbows we fish, those are simply empty boats.

We have an invention that was made from an old trolling motor bracket, an old license plate (Arkansas preferably), a couple of small one-inch long screws, and a piece of three quarter inch PVC. You put that all together and hang it over the back of the boat and it works like magic.

If you leave home and realize you have forgotten said magic, you must improvise. One day we found an empty 3-liter drink bottle. We filled it about two thirds full and tied it just behind the back of the boat. Magic! Another day, no one had been polite enough to leave a 3-liter bottle, so we tied a short thick log on the back. Magic!

That brings to mind an old saying from the deep south; *A poor man has poor ways.* Or as my nephew told me after sending him a picture of the log tied to the back of the boat: *A stupid man has stupid ways.* I could not argue.

Shocking Fish(erman) - I told the story in my fishing adventure book about three teenagers who attempted to shock the fish in a pond using an antique phone with a crank handle. They were young and stupid and certainly did not know what they were doing. After shocking themselves repeatedly, they pitched the apparatus into the pond and walked away. Two of them continued to say %#*#$! multiple times as they were walking away. The other did not as his mother would never allow that kind of language to be spoken.

As I said, those three were amateurs. My grandfather on the other hand, was a pro at shocking fish. Back about 1976 he started taking me fishing with him. To him, fishing meant setting out a trot line and a few yo yos. This would be followed by motoring back to the truck and commencing to drink up every bottle of liquor he had brought. He would then pass out and I would be left to run the trot line and yo yos. This was okay as I enjoyed pulling in the fish we caught. Then the next morning I would take everything up and drive him back home where my grandmother would tear into him for getting drunk again. Sometimes I would wonder why he wanted to get drunk. Oh well, maybe he deserved chewing out.

On one of these trips, he taught me something new. He pulled his truck up to the water's edge. We popped the hood. He retrieved an old window weight with electrical wire attached from the bed of his truck. It seemed to be about fifty feet worth of double wire. He then drove a horseshoe stake into the shore right at the water line. He attached one of the wires to that and attached the other to his number one plug on his V-8 pickup. He cranked up the motor and revved it up! Fish in the area began to surface rapidly. He had instructed me to be ready to jump into the boat and paddle out quick as soon as he killed the motor. I was netting fish left and right. It was exciting for a few minutes but I learned quickly that proper fishing is done with a rod and reel, so I never tried that one again.

I've heard that the only thing more accomplished at catching fish is dynamite. I'm kind of glad me and my buddies never had any, I feel certain we would have given it a go.

Stump Jumper - If you fish as many old river lakes as we have, this is what your boat turns into. You better make sure you have the heavy-duty aluminum boat.
And this can also lead to losing the motor off the back of

the boat four times. (See Terry's fishing adventure book.)

Tumped over - Most know this term to mean when you turn over your wheel barrel that was previously loaded with dirt, or cement, or any other heavy material.
The proper usage of the term references your boat as you have leaned over too far to net a fish, gig a frog, hang a dreaded yo yo, or many other actions that may cause the boat to lean too far to one side.

And yes, my friends would always say %#*#$! after I tumped the boat over with them in it, again!

About the Author

Terry lives in the Martindale community in western Pulaski County in central Arkansas. That would be just south of Ferndale and a little east of Moody Holler. He grew up fishing along McHenry Creek with his brothers and friends.

Terry developed a passion for fishing and was soon recognized as a little excitable and careless with his love for the outdoors. As he grew into manhood, many of his fishing and hunting trips turned into adventures. Terry began taking notes.

His supernatural ability for ending up in hospitals or clinics from injuries while fishing and hunting has made him infamous locally. People have been urging him to write a book for years. "I guess having had twenty trips to an emergency room, twenty broken bones, one hundred stitches, four concussions, and one bite from a cottonmouth moccasin is enough to write home about."

Terry is the training director for SET Environmental out of the Little Rock office. He conducts safety training with workers from over one hundred workplaces each year. He is known as the Safety Guy. His knack for storytelling and communication skills get him invited to speak at eighteen to twenty annual conferences and conventions each year.

He has been married to his special friend, Carla, for over thirty-seven years. They have two daughters: Amanda, thirty-one, who lives in Jacksonville, Florida, and

Mikayla, twenty-two, who lives in North Hollywood, California. None of which hunt or fish, having seen the results of Terry's many adventures, and want none of that.

After noticing devastating ads on TV, and realizing both of his daughters are healthy, he has donated his hair five times over the past nine years to organizations that help young girls with cancer.

If you enjoyed *Up McHenry Creek Without a Paddle*:

Please consider checking out my latest title!

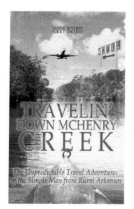

Traveling for Terry Bryant is an unpredictable adventure...or misadventure rather.

The business of training people on how to be safe in their work environment has taken him near and far. He has run the gamut in his attitude from being angry about the randomness of traveling to savoring the variety.

At some point, among the urine-soaked mattresses, two to be exact, and unexpected naked ladies in his room, Terry found a way to experience joy in the unpredictable nature of air travel and budget motels.

In addition, Terry has survived a knife fight, been detained at a military base, and managed to navigate an uncomfortable confrontation with a couple of booze-soaked honeymooners.

Terry's stories both delight and empower. From the first chapter, you will gain a new, positive perspective from a man who turns the strife of life into a wild and exciting adventure.

Do not miss these, and many more fun and hilarious stories courtesy of the simple man from rural Arkansas.

Grab it on your favorite reading platform by clicking this link - http://mchenrycreekfishers.com/travelingmchenrycreek

Made in the USA
Columbia, SC
17 August 2019